WINERIES
& WINE COUNTRY OF
NOVA SCOTIA

SEAN P. WOOD

NIMBUS
PUBLISHING

Nimbus Publishing Limited
PO Box 9166, Halifax, NS B3K 5M8
(902) 455 -4286

Printed and bound in Canada

Design: Neil Meister, Semaphor Design Company Inc.

Front cover: Gaspereau Vineyards

Title page: Dr. Allan McIntyre's vineyard, Canning, NS

Library and Archives Canada Cataloguing in Publication

    Wood Sean P.
    Wineries and wine country of Nova Scotia / Sean P. Wood.
    Includes index.
    ISBN 1-55109-573-4

1. Wineries—Nova Scotia—Guidebooks. 2. Wine and wine making—Nova Scotia. 3. Nova Scotia—Guidebooks. I. Title.

TP559.C3W66 2006   663'.2009716
C2006-901499-X

We acknowledge the financial support of the Government of Canada through the Book Publishing Industry Development Program (BPIDP) and the Canada Council, and of the Province of Nova Scotia through the Department of Tourism, Culture and Heritage for our publishing activities.

ACKNOWLEDGMENTS

Most books are a collaborative effort and this one, more so than most. I wish to thank the many people who have contributed time, skill and knowledge in bringing it to publication. The Winery Association of Nova Scotia assisted in so many ways. Martha Reynolds, of the association, was particularly helpful in providing much important information that found its way into these pages. The individual wineries could not have been more cooperative in providing everything that I asked of them.

There is a bright future for the wines of Nova Scotia, which I hope this little volume will help to highlight. The wines have never been better and their distinctive regional qualities are more evident with every vintage. As I set out to write the book, I knew that the story would be even more compelling as seen through the images that excited me as I travelled around the wine country. The stunning photographs speak for themselves and I owe my thanks to all who contributed, especially Anita MacPherson of AMac Photography, Christopher Ball, and Sheila Ferguson of the NS Department of Agriculture and Fisheries.

I am also deeply grateful to the board and management of the Nova Scotia Liquor Corporation for their encouragement and support of this project.

Lastly, I would like to thank the able and hardworking staff of Nimbus Publishing. No author could have asked for a more pleasant professional relationship.

Table of Contents

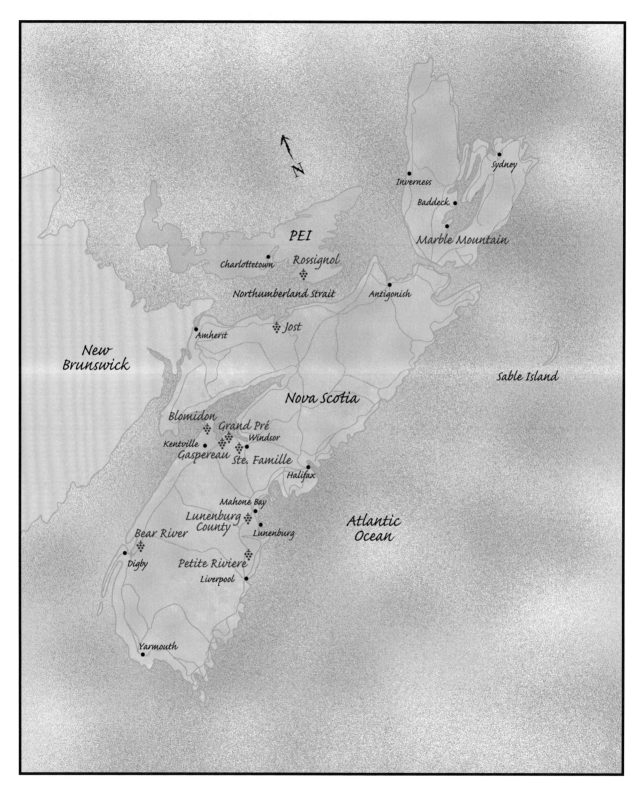

Introduction

Nova Scotia is arguably the oldest wine-producing region in North America. As far back as the early 1630s, the commander of the French colony at LaHave on the province's south shore, Isaac de Razilly, wrote to Marc Lescarbot in Paris of the success of his Nova Scotia vineyard, planted with cuttings from Bordeaux. In the 1760s, New England Planters settled the Annapolis Valley, and the Planter women—who often acted as the family brewmaster—stored many kinds of wines, as well as apple cider and spruce beer, in their cellars.

Despite this historical precedent for wine production, serious wine production in Nova Scotia revived only in the 1970s and 1980s. Wine pioneer Roger Dial opened the first commercial winery, Grand Pré, in the Annapolis Valley in the early 1980s. It is an expensive proposition to establish a successful winery, especially in a new wine-growing region like Nova Scotia was at the time. Once a suitable vineyard site has been identified and the vines planted, it takes several years before those vines can produce harvestable grapes in commercial quantities. Add to this the necessary investment in wine-making equipment—wine presses, fermentation vats, barrels, bottling lines and the like—and it requires many years before a winemaker can expect a return on that investment. Seeing this as a serious obstacle, Dial persuaded the Nova Scotia government of the day to establish a favourable farm winery

Vinifera (*Vitis vinifera*): the classic
European family of grapes which include
the world's most famous (and most
respected) varieties. The best known are
the whites: Chardonnay, Sauvignon
Blanc, Riesling and Chenin Blanc and
the reds: Cabernet Sauvignon, Merlot,
Pinot Noir and Shiraz/Syrah.

VALLEY WINE TOURS

In 2005, enterprising young sommeliers
and Nova Scotia wine enthusiasts Mark
DeWolf and Sean Buckland established
"Valley Wine Tours." Departing from
downtown Halifax in a fourteen-passen-
ger air-conditioned van, this unique
service offers expertly guided day tours
of the principal wineries and vineyards
of the Annapolis Valley. The leisurely
program also includes tastings at three
wineries and a gourmet lunch with
appropriately paired Nova Scotia wines.

For more information:
info@valleywinetours.ca;
1-866-504-9463.

policy, arguing that setting up a viable wine industry
would utimately be beneficial to the province. The policy permitted wineries with grapes under cultivation in
Nova Scotia to import and sell wine sourced from grapes
grown elsewhere. This provided both a supply of product and the necessary cash flow to support the development of local wine growing. In 1983, shortly after Dial's
Grand Pré winery opened, Hans Jost, originally from
Germany's Rhineland region, opened a winery at
Malagash on the Northumberland Strait. Jost Vineyards,
managed today by Hans Christian Jost, son of founder
Hans, is Nova Scotia's longest-established winery as well
as its largest. While Dial's original Grand Pré did not
survive, his winery was spectacularly revived under the
leadership of Swiss banker Hanspeter Stutz. The new
Domaine de Grand Pré has become Nova Scotia's showpiece winery and has significantly raised the bar for
overall quality.

Across the province on its south shore, the Petite
Rivière Vineyards and Winery benefits from the LaHave
River Valley's distinctive landscape, which is dotted with
small rounded hills known as drumlins. These glacial
deposits composed of sand, gravel, and broken slate

Roger Dial's original Grand Pré winery, 1987.

soil provide excellent natural drainage and low vigour. The area also benefits from sheltered south-facing slopes and proximity to the moderating influence of the nearby Atlantic Ocean, making the valley the mildest wine-growing region east of the Niagara Peninsula. The winery's opening has also meant that, in a sense, history has come full circle: it is but a few miles from where de Razilly planted his grapes over three centuries ago.

History has also repeated itself at another known site of an original seventeenth-century vineyard. Some years ago, Chris Hawes, who caught the wine bug while working as a student in the Niagara vineyards, set about planting grapes on his property at Bear River close to the Annapolis Basin, where French settlers are known to have planted grapes three hundred and fifty years earlier. Before Hawes began planting, Nova Scotia's wine culture had been based almost exclusively on winter-hardy French-American hybrid varieties. Most growers and winemakers had concluded that the climate was too harsh for the more tender viniferas. Surprisingly, although Hawes has planted some hybrids, most of his small acreage is devoted to viniferas. Even more remarkable, these viniferas continue to thrive even through severe winters. Today, his largest single planting is Pinot Noir, with Chardonnay, Riesling, Pinot Gris, and Auxerrois also doing well.

Perhaps it makes more sense for Nova Scotia's wine regions to be compared to the cool-climate regions of Germany rather than to other parts of continental North America, since continental weather patterns are offset, to a considerable

Drumlin—broken slatey soil left behind by retreating glaciers

extent, by the moderating influences of the Atlantic Ocean. If the expansive Annapolis Valley can be broadly compared to the Rhine, the smaller, meandering Gaspereau Valley bears a similar resemblance to the Mosel. Roger Dial believed Gaspereau held immense potential as a grape-growing region. It took some time before vineyards were established in this valley, but there are now several thriving vineyards planted and the first winery, Gaspereau Vineyards, opened its doors in 2004. The quality of fruit coming from the Gaspereau seems to be bearing out Dial's prediction. Sainte Famille, a long-established small cottage winery near Falmouth at the gateway to the Annapolis Valley, is also thriving. Blomidon Estate Winery, under the same ownership as Niagara's Creekside, replanted much of its vineyard in recent years and is producing small quantities of greatly improved wine.

Lunenburg County Winery, on Nova Scotia's south shore, is almost exclusively devoted to fruit, utilizing a wide variety of berries and tree fruit as well as maple and, most recently, Nova Scotia-grown arctic kiwi fruit.

John Pratt's Marble Mountain vineyard—spectacular Cape Breton scenery

Perhaps the most spectacular, and certainly the most northerly, vineyard in Nova Scotia is at Marble Mountain in Cape Breton. Planted by American businessman John Pratt, known locally as "Johnny Grape," the vineyard, sheltered from the prevailing winds by the mass of Marble Mountain, sweeps gracefully downward towards the Bras d'Or Lake. The Bras d'Or is actually an inland sea which rarely freezes, greatly moderating winter temperatures. Spring comes late here, but autumn is also prolonged, and this is often the last vineyard in the province to experience frost. There is no winery of yet in Cape Breton. At present, Pratt's grapes are made into wine under the Jost label.

Rossignol Estate, Prince Edward Island's lone commercial winery, also enjoys a spectacular setting overlooking the Northumberland Strait. Founder and winemaker John Rossignol works with both fruit and hybrid grapes and has recently released a wine which he refers to as a "forbidden marriage" between blueberry and the hybrid grape, Marechal Foch. He has also

Highbush blueberries

Ice wine grapes covered with protective netting

grown vinifera varieties in protected greenhouses, but has recently abandoned that experiment.

Overall, though, the number of commercial wineries in the province remains small. In fact, the industry's leading challenge in the next few years is to increase the critical mass of both vineyards and wineries. Along the length of the Annapolis Valley's North Mountain alone, there are literally thousands of acres suitable for vineyard cultivation. While Nova Scotia still only has a few hundred acres under vine, the province has greater unrealized potential than either Ontario or British Columbia. Since the early 1980s when skeptics thought it impossible to develop a wine culture in Nova Scotia, there have been numerous developments that have made the idea increasingly viable. Arguably the two most important innovations are new grape clones that have been developed to ripen faster and to withstand colder temperatures, and malolactic fermentation tech-

niques and new yeast strains that can reduce excess acidity associated with cold climate.

For Nova Scotia the future looks very promising; several new wineries are planned in the next two to three years, including two in the Gaspereau Valley alone. Winemakers and growers have learned how to get impressive results from signature local varieties such as the crisp, fruity white, l'Acadie Blanc, and the highly aromatic New York Muscat. These two, together with Seyval Blanc, pair extremely well with local seafood. Icewines, made from Vidal, New York Muscat, Ortega, and other varieties, are already among Canada's best. The workhorse red, Marechal Foch, produces steady, reliable quality in most vintages, but other red hybrids like Leon Millot and, particularly, Baco Noir, promise to be much better. Vinifera varieties planted in vineyards with favourable microclimates are showing that Chardonnay, Pinot Noir, and Riesling can all play a part in the future of the region.

THE NEW NOVA SCOTIA WINE STANDARDS

The Nova Scotia Wine Standards (NSWS) are new standards that enable consumers to identify quality grape wines of Nova Scotia, based on the origin of the grapes from which they are produced. With the new regulations, Nova Scotia joins other leading wine-producing provinces and countries in developing a body of standards for its grape wines. Wineries are entitled to use the provincial designation—Nova Scotia—on the principal display panel of a bottle, provided not less than eighty-five per cent of the wine's content is derived from grapes grown within the province and meets all standards such as minimum brix (ripeness) levels, alcohol content, and the like. Unlike the existing Vintners Quality Alliance (VQA) in Ontario and British Columbia, the Nova Scotia wine standard does not permit the addition of water under any circumstances.

The Nova Scotia Wine Standards resulted from the recommendations of the Nova Scotia Wine Standards Committee, an open committee comprised of wineries belonging to The Winery Association of Nova Scotia, with representation from the Grape Growers Association of Nova Scotia and the Nova Scotia government. The standards apply only to wines that display the Nova Scotia Geographical Indicator (NSGI) on the bottle's principal display panel. Ice wines, all late harvest wines, botrytized wines, and vin de curé are required to display the NSGI on the principal display panel and must meet these standards. All other wines have the option to display the NSGI on the principal display panel if they meet these standards. Wines that are not required or choose not to display the NSGI on the principal display panel are not covered by these standards.

The Wines of Nova Scotia quality symbol was created by the Winery Association of Nova Scotia to identify quality wines made from one hundred per cent Nova Scotia grapes. The symbol—a lobster claw holding a tilting glass of wine—is designed to symbolize the distinctive character of wines made with Nova Scotia grown grapes. It can only be used by wineries that are in good standing with the Winery Association of Nova Scotia, meet the Nova Scotia Wine Standards, and whose wine content is one hundred per cent derived from Nova Scotia-grown grapes. Of note is that fruit wines may carry the logo on packaging as well, provided they meet the one hundred per cent local content rules. A related program is a marketing initiative of the Winery Association. Member wineries of the association can enter into a licensing agreement that permits them to use the logo/trademark on their packaging.

In creating these standards, the Nova Scotia wine industry has laid the essential ground work for this province to be recognized as a truly credible, high-quality, authentic wine-producing region in its own right.

Nova Scotia Tastes and Benchmark Grapes

Wine can, of course, be enjoyed as a straightforward, simple pleasure. Many wines are undemanding beverages to be appreciated as you would a glass of beer or cider. For those who want to go a little further, however, a whole new world of sensory experience is available. Everyone understands that it is necessary to train our eyesight to perform complex tasks such as reading, and attune our hearing in order to grasp the meaning of conversation or music. It does not occur to most of us, however, to think about paying similar attention to the senses of taste and smell.

The most important thing to appreciate is that what we think of as "taste" is mostly derived from the sense of smell. The mouth actually picks up only four basic "tastes": sweetness, saltiness, acidity (sourness), and bitterness. Arguably, you could add one more, the sensation of peppery spice. By comparison, our olfactory sense can discern literally thousands of different sensations. Without the sense of smell, we can taste practically nothing.

When tasting wines, trust your own taste first. Do not be persuaded by other opinions if they contradict your own impressions. Secondly, avoid distraction. Tasting properly, like acquiring any skill, requires a bit of concentration. The better the wine, the more it will demand your attention. Thirdly, the room should be free of other distracting smells; perfumes, tobacco smoke, and strong food aromas all interfere with the ability to taste.

Perhaps the best advice I have received is to let the wine talk to you. Ask questions like, "Is this wine good or bad?" and "Do I like this wine?" Then you should try to answer the further question "If so, why? If not, why not?" Taking notes can give you a record of your impressions and will help you to remember the kind of wines you enjoy and the ones you do not.

When it comes to Nova Scotia wines, it's good to remember that they have their own very distinct characterisics. As growers and winemakers have come to understand the soils, climatic conditions, and grape varieties that they have to work with, the wines have come to reflect the local terroir more definitively. Nova Scotia wines today are much better than they were in the past, and certain grape varieties have even emerged as "signature" wines for the region.

In Nova Scotia's cool climatic conditions, the whites, so far at least, have continued to outshine the reds. Like they do in Germany, the best whites reveal intensely aromatic, vibrantly fresh fruit with crisp, lively acidity. These wines pair perfectly with the excellent local seafood. The reds do well with a variety of local foods including most red meats and firm-ripened cheeses. Beginning with chef Michael Smith's efforts at Halifax's Maple Restaurant, local chefs have

Hybrids: the term usually refers to grape varieties developed from native North American and vinifera varieties to withstand harsher winter conditions while still providing a good flavour profile.

The use of oak/oak aging: oak is used to soften and add complexity to certain wines, most often, but not exclusively, reds. New oak will impart more oaky flavours, while older barrels will help age the wine while adding less oaky character. The most common types of oak are French (most expensive) and American. Today, however, we are seeing more Hungarian, Slovenian and even a very small amount of Canadian oak (only in Niagara). The poor man's version is to put wood chips into stainless steel tanks, thus producing some similar effects. In some cases, wood-stave frames are erected within such tanks.

created a wide range of memorable menus pairing Nova Scotia wines with the region's cuisine.

Nova Scotia reds also show aromatic characteristics, somewhat akin to the red wines of the Loire in France and sometimes resembling the fresh fruity style of Beaujolais. Acidity in these wines can be quite pronounced and tends to be a bit green in poorer vintages. This has been much less evident in recent years as growers have learned to use better techniques in the vineyard and new technology in the winemaking process. "Green harvesting," or the practice of cutting away a certain number of clusters on each vine, concentrates more of the vine's energy into fewer grapes, making for more concentrated and riper fruit. Overall yield will of course be lower, but the reward in higher quality more than makes up for it. The use of new strains of yeast and different fermentation techniques in the winery have done wonders in reducing excess acidity.

Barring dramatic climate change, Nova Scotia will never produce big, blockbuster-style reds but, especially in good years, grapes like Baco Noir can produce quite robust full-bodied wines. Reserve quality oak-aged Marechal Foch can also be substantial and generous on the palate.

Wine tasting obviously can involve more complex technical skills, but with the following guidelines in mind, anyone can develop a more discerning palate and increase his or her enjoyment of wine.

Glasses should be large, bowl-shaped, and tapered towards the aperture. The ideal glass is clear with a large enough bowl to permit swirling, which aerates or "breathes" the wine. Swirling also increases the wine's surface area, intensifying scent. The glass is also tapered towards the brim in order to concentrate the fullness of the bouquet. The classic tulip-shaped Bordeaux glass is the most adaptable style, and works well with both red and white wines. Handle glasses by the stem (only hold the bowl in order to warm the wine if necessary). As a general rule, most red wines should be served between 16-18 degrees Celsius. Lighter reds can be served a little cooler. Most dry whites and rosés should be served at 8-10 degrees Celsius. Most sweet white and sparkling wines should be served at 3-7 degrees Celsius (standard refrigerator temperature).

A room with good natural light provides the best environment for tasting; however, using a candle and examining the wine against a white tablecloth also works quite well. First study the appearance of the wine. Look for clarity and brightness, depth and vividness of colour. Faulted wines may show signs of cloudiness, browning, or dullness. Take note that some wines are bottled unfiltered, in which case some cloudiness caused by sediment is not a fault. The wine should be placed upright allowing the sediment to fall to the bottom and then be carefully decanted before serving.

Sniff close to the glass. Breathe in for a brief moment or two and then sniff again (otherwise your nose can quickly become tired and confused). When tasting, take a sip and circulate it around the mouth—"chew it." Slurp the wine (politely, of course). Aerating the wine in this way enhances and brings back the smell. After swallowing, breathe out through your nose. This will bring out the aftertaste or "finish."

THE BENCHMARK GRAPES

Whites

L'Acadie Blanc (official name L'Acadie): Christened by Roger Dial in the 1970s, this hybrid variety was first developed at the Vineland research station in Ontario's Niagara region but never thrived in that province. When planted here, it quickly established itself as Nova Scotia's workhorse white variety. It can show wonderfully crisp

Typical smaller wine tasting glasses have wider bowls and narrow towards aperature

L'Acadie Blanc

New York Muscat

Seyval Blanc

Vidal

green apple fruit with vibrant acidity and some mineral character. It is also capable of aging quite well and can resemble Chardonnay when more mature.

L'Acadie Blanc can also be made successfully with some barrel aging. This gives the wine a bit more weight on the palate and adds some complexity. Like most Nova Scotia whites, though, it shows its finest pure fruit qualities in a straightforward unoaked style. It matches very well with seafood and white meat dishes, particularly oysters on the half-shell. If given my choice between Muscadet, the dry white from the Loire often served with this dish, and L'Acadie Blanc, I would choose the latter every time.

New York Muscat: First named by the New York Research Station in 1961, this highly aromatic white variety has become uniquely Nova Scotian. The distinguished Swiss oenologist Valentin Blattner, when tasting this wine in 2004, said, "No one else in the world is making wine like this. It should become the signature grape for your region." The bouquet is intense with floral blossom, fresh green fruit, herbal and sometimes lightly peppery overtones. On the palate, its characteristic flavours are lively green fruit, crisp minerality, some lychee and hints of white pepper. It pairs superbly with seafood dishes prepared with some Oriental spiciness. Together with Vidal (see below), New York Muscat also makes some of the province's best ice wine and late harvest dessert wines.

Seyval Blanc: Another winter-hardy French-American hybrid, Seyval Blanc grows successfully elsewhere in eastern North America and England. It does quite well in Nova Scotia, making fairly neutral crisp, dry, light wines and a somewhat more distinctive off-dry style.

Vidal: A late-ripening hybrid which has been used to make both dry and sweet wines. Vidal, which thrives in Canada (including Nova Scotia), has reached its zenith in ice wine. The tough-skinned grapes not only

Young vines being cultivated in the nursery

develop voluptuous aromas and flavours, but also manage to cling to the vines and resist rot for a long time after the normal harvest. These exceptionally complex, powerful wines are now recognized as some of the finest dessert wines in the world.

Chardonnay: Initially thought to be insufficiently winter hardy for Nova Scotia, this classic white grape has now been planted in several different parts of the province. There have been several commercial releases over the last couple of years, although so far in relatively small quantities. Early results show promise with lighter-bodied wines showing green apple cleanness on the palate.

Riesling, various Riesling crosses: Riesling and various crosses developed at Geisenheim, Germany, and locally have been planted in Nova Scotia with varying degrees of success. Experiments continue, and high quality winter-hardy Germanic styles will clearly play an important role in the future.

Ortega: A cross between the German varieties Muller-Thurgau and Siegerrebe frequently used for

Chardonnay

Riesling

Siegfried

blending. A winter-hardy variety, it has shown great finesse when made into ice wine in Nova Scotia.

Reds

Marechal Foch: A well-established French-American hybrid also grown in Ontario and British Columbia, Marechal Foch is a steady, reliable performer and the most widely planted red grape in Nova Scotia. It can be made in both lighter and fuller-bodied styles and also benefits from oak aging. At its best it can show some Burgundian roundness. More often, though, it has dark cherry flavours and pronounced herbal notes, not unlike young Beaujolais or Italian Sangiovese.

Leon Millot: A later arrival on the scene than Marechal Foch, Leon Millot was developed in Alsace and has shown itself to be particularly well-suited to this region. Its flavour is more akin to higher quality vinifera varieties and it ripens well in most vintages.

Lucy Kuhlmann: An early ripening hybrid closely resembling Marechal Foch. It has good colour and body with attractive fruity qualities and a pronounced herbal character.

Baco Noir: Another fairly recent arrival in Nova Scotia, this hybrid has done very well in Niagara and local growers seem to be learning how to handle it in this region. Baco is dark and full-bodied with plenty of dark fruit, good structure, and a hint of smokiness. It improves with oak aging and pairs well with robust red-meat dishes. It appears destined to become one of the region's best red varieties.

Pinot Noir: Variously described as wine's Holy Grail or, more frequently, "the heartbreak grape," Pinot Noir is a low producer and rarely achieves its full potential, even in its native Burgundy. Nonetheless, it is the dream of ambitious winemakers in all cool climate regions to make a great Pinot Noir. Nova Scotia is no exception. It has been planted in several places around the province

Marechal Foch

Leon Millot

Lucy Kuhlmann

Baco Noir

Pinot Noir

De Chaunac

with mixed results. There have been a couple of small quantities released commercially, but as of publication, some early optimism has yet to be born out. Pinot Noir is one of the three grapes that make up the classic blend for Champagne. Currently, there are plans underway to make high-quality, Champagne-style sparkling wines in the Gaspereau Valley region. It may be in this way that the grape will play its most valuable role in the future.

De Chaunac: De Chaunac is a red variety that has shown promising results in Nova Scotia. It can be

Tending vines in the Gaspereau Valley's Benjamin Bridge vineyard

quite intense, showing herbal freshness and notes of bell peppers, ripe plums, and dark cherries.

Roger Dial brought in several winter-hardy Russian varieties such as Michurinetz and Severnyi. Although difficult to work with, these varieties can make surprisingly good wine and, despite their exasperating tendencies, winemakers still persevere with them. In the search for winter hardiness combined with good flavour profiles, a number of other varieties have been planted, but have yet to make a major impact. More recently, various vinifera varieties have been planted in different sites around Nova Scotia and have fared reasonably well over the recent winters. In Chris Hawes's Bear River vineyard in southwest Nova Scotia, the vinifera varieties Pinot Noir, Chardonnay, Pinot Blanc, Auxerrois, and Riesling have been planted and have survived over several years.

JOST VINEYARDS
Nova Scotia's Oldest and Largest Winery

A long the Sunrise Trail in northern Nova Scotia, the sparkling warm waters of the Northumberland Strait welcome visitors from near and far. The area's beaches are renowned for their relative warmth, lobster and waterfowl are plentiful, and crumbling brick-red cliffs and sand dunes give the impression that Prince Edward Island is nearby. French settlers first colonized the region but Scottish settlers established permanent settlements, especially in Pictou and Antigonish

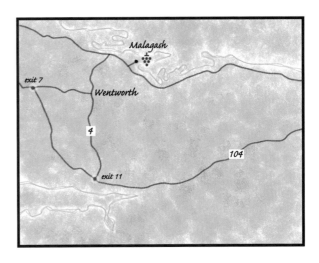

The 2005 Vintage in Nova Scotia

The 2005 growing season got off to a very bad start with another cold, damp, and late spring. Things were looking gloomy until mid-summer, whereupon the weather took a turn for the better, with dry warm days and relatively warm nights as well. As harvest time drew closer, growers were collectively holding their breath, as an almost miraculously warm, dry weather persisted through late August and early September. This enabled the grapes to make up for lost time as they continued to ripen well, especially as overnight temperatures remained warm.

When harvested, earlier-ripening varieties showed mature fruit at healthy sugar levels and will produce solid wines, likely well above average quality. Ever capricious, though, Mother Nature saw fit to rain on the parade in October. Those who waited too long found fruit intensity diluted by heavy downpours before harvesting. In some sites, birds, knowing exactly when the fruit had ripened, descended on the vineyards and helped themselves to a large share of the crop. These losses will reduce the overall volume somewhat, but on balance 2005 is turning out to be a very solid vintage.

Counties. Maple sugar and blueberries are major export products and the Sugar Moon Farm and Pancake House at Earltown is now a major tourist attraction with its famous traditional maple suppers served year-round. As well, the Wild Blueberry & Maple Centre at Oxford offers a wide-ranging introduction to maple and blueberry production as well as advice on cooking with them.

Here, just a stone's throw from the Northumberland Strait on the Malagash peninsula, is the beautifully situated Jost Vineyards. Hans Jost emigrated with his family to Canada in 1970 from Germany, where he had owned and operated a winery and vineyards in the Rhine Valley. The Jost family involvement with winemaking goes back some three hundred years, so it is perhaps not surprising that the family would turn their hands to viticulture in their adopted homeland. Initially, though, they started making wine for their own use and only later saw the possibility of establishing a viable commercial winery. The Jost enterprise got underway in 1983, and today is a thriving operation that attracts some 40,000 visitors annually. Although somewhat off the beaten track, there are well-marked signposts from the Trans-Canada Highway that direct you to the winery gate.

Since Hans's death a number of years ago, his son Hans Christian has been running the winery. He has continued, to a great extent, in the German tradition of winemaking that Hans espoused. He is fond of quoting his father's assertion that "the wine should taste of the grape, not the container." According to this way of thinking, the winemaker's objective should be to impart all the clean, fresh, and authentic flavour of the fruit with a minimum of "foreign" influences. It is the very opposite of the heavily oak-influenced wines of California and Australia that have become so

TASTING NOTES

L'ACADIE BLANC, 2003 $12.99

L'Acadie Blanc is Nova Scotia's signature white grape variety, making clean and refreshingly light wines that pair exceptionally well with local seafood. This one shows citrus and green apple scents with a hint of vanilla and attractive citrus and crisp peach flavours on the palate. Dry and well-balanced, it finishes with a smooth touch of oak.

EAGLE TREE MUSCAT, 2003 $14.99

Highly aromatic, showing floral blossom, citrus, and lychee, as well as some mineral on the nose, this wine has zesty green fruit flavours with some spicy character and crisp acidity. Sappy green fruit and lychee linger on the palate. Matches well with fresh seafood and spicy oriental salads.

LIMITED EDITION LEON MILLOT, 2003 $13.99

This red variety has a spicy cherry bouquet with a light smoky overtone. Flavours of sweet ripe cherry have some added spicy and lightly peppery notes with rounded tannins, though youthful acidity is still prominent. Finishing with black cherry and spice, it makes a good match for red meat dishes, tomato-based pastas, and firm cheeses.

Hans Jost

popular. It is also appropriate to many of the grape varieties that thrive in Nova Scotia. There are many parallels in the climatic challenges posed to both German and Nova Scotian winemakers. The German experience is, therefore, a useful model for winemaking in this province.

Hans Christian is, however, also a pragmatist. He is willing to experiment and to learn by his mistakes. He admits, with disarming candour, that some of his greatest successes have been accidental. What he enjoys about winemaking is its variety, the opportunity to get out from behind a desk and to try new things around the vines and in the winery itself. Two years ago, he began using a limited amount of oak with, I believe, very favourable results. The winery started with eighteen barrels of three-year-old French Limousin oak. Used oak imparts less "oakiness" than new oak, so the results are more subtle. Encouraged by the results so far, the winery will shortly acquire thirty-eight more barrels, thus tripling current capacity. Particularly in Nova Scotia's cool climate, some grape varieties can produce rather sharp and acidic wines. Oak aging can help soften and round out such wines, making them more attractive.

As in Germany, winegrowers need to seek out "microclimates" around the province that enjoy particularly favourable conditions, such as south facing, well-protected slopes not exposed to early frost. This is a time-consuming, trial-and-error process. As Hans Christian says, "If we had known ten years ago what we know today, we would be twenty years ahead." At

Hans Christian Jost and Jost winemaker David Beardsall

TASTING NOTES

BACO NOIR, 2003 $19.99

Bouquet shows elegant dark berry fruit with some savoury and herbal notes. In the mouth, flavours of bitter cherry, plum, and cranberry are backed up by firm tannic structure and plenty of acidity. Finishing with bitter cherry and dry spice, this is a wine of some style that will drink well with grilled red meats, especially lamb chops and hard-ripened cheeses. Best with three-to-five years additional time in the cellar.

TRILOGY, 2003 $17.99

This blend of Baco Noir, Leon Millot, and Marechal Foch aged in French oak is a new departure for Nova Scotia and a notable success. Good depth of berry and black cherry fruit with lightly peppery notes and a hint of dark chocolate on the palate. The wine is evolving towards a smooth velvet texture; it shows well-integrated fruit, spice, and a mellow touch of oak on the finish.

Jost tasting room and winery store

present, Jost has forty-five acres of grapes under cultivation at the Malagash vineyard. The winery obtains a significant proportion of its fruit from other growers, including from vineyards situated in the Annapolis Valley, Bridgewater and Marble Mountain in Cape Breton. Jost also uses grapes from outside Nova Scotia for many of its blended and everyday quality wines—the wines seen most often on liquor store shelves. The higher quality estate wines and individual vineyard wines, drawn exclusively from Nova Scotian vineyards, are normally only sold directly from the winery. This provides another good reason for making the trip to the Malagash-based vineyard located just off the Sunrise Trail.

Today, Jost Vineyards boasts an attractive wine store, tasting room and snack bar with a licensed patio. There is even a barbeque for visitors' use. Like the Niagara region before it, Nova Scotia is beginning to develop its own distinctive styles, capitalizing on the unique characteristics of soil and climate. As Hans Christian says: "In the past our wines were

Jody Wood's Nova Scotia Icewine Mousse

4 egg yolks

4 egg whites

1 cup sugar

1/2 cup Nova Scotia Icewine (preferably New York Muscat, but Vidal, or Ortega-based Icewines will also work perfectly)

1 envelope plain gelatin

1/4 cup cold water

1 cup whipping cream

Unsweetened chocolate for garnish

Beat yolks and half the sugar until light and lemon coloured, then add icewine.

Sprinkle gelatin on cold water; microwave for one minute to dissolve. Stir into egg yolk mixture. Beat cream until stiff and moist. Add remaining sugar slowly. Fold cream into egg yolk mixture, then fold in stiffly beaten egg whites. Pour into serving dish. Garnish with shaved chocolate.

Chill 4-6 hours. Top with whipped cream if desired.

Serve with a glass of the icewine used for the mousse.

compared to other parts of the world, now we are being compared to our earlier wines, other Nova Scotian wines or other Canadian wines." With his wife Karen, Hans Christian also established Gaspereau Valley Vineyards in 2004 on fifty acres of beautiful property just outside Wolfville.

Hours:

May 1–Christmas: daily
Christmas–April 30: Monday–Saturday

Tours at 12 p.m. and 3 p.m. daily

Location: 48 Vintage Lane, Malagash

Contact: 1-800-565-4567
www.jostwine.com
info@jostwine.com

Winemakers: Hans Christian Jost
and David Beardsall

SAINTE FAMILLE WINES
Small is Beautiful

Located roughly three miles outside present-day Falmouth near Windsor, this small, family-owned vineyard and winery is situated on the site of an Acadian village. The name "Sainte Famille" harks back to the original parish known as "Saint Famille de Pisiquit," which was settled around 1685. There are no visible remains of the early settlement but the vineyard is pleasantly situated on a gently sloping hill looking out over open country towards Ski Martock.

Sainte Famille is the inspiration of Suzanne Corkum, who hails from the Willamette Valley in Oregon. Suzanne's family farmed that fertile region, producing mostly strawberries. Her father, of German descent, had created a small vineyard over the years. In those days, however, Oregon was considered too cold to become a serious wine-producing area and her

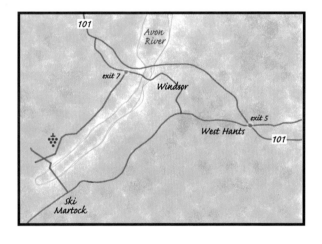

father's vineyard was little more than a harmless hobby. Today, of course, Oregon, and particularly the Willamette Valley, has become an important challenger for top honours in the American wine world. Little wonder, then, that Suzanne was undaunted by the prospect of growing grapes in the even more improbable locale of Nova Scotia.

When circumstances brought Suzanne to Nova Scotia, she was interested in trying her hand at farming, and subsequently she and husband Doug acquired their present property. Around 1980, Suzanne saw an article on Roger Dial's successful work at Grand Pré. After meeting him, she was sufficiently encouraged to plant wine grapes herself. The following year she planted one acre of the French-American hybrid grape, Marechal Foch, and over the next year or so added an acre of Chardonnay and another acre planted with the Russian variety Michurinetz. In the 1980s, Sainte Famille was strictly a vineyard supplying grapes to the Grand Pré winery. Later in the

decade, Suzanne and Doug began to seriously consider establishing their own winery. She discussed the idea with Alan Schmidt, wine-maker at Vineland Estates in Ontario. Schmidt told her to "come out and help me for a harvest and afterwards decide if you want to do it." Having survived the experience, Suzanne decided to go ahead with her own winery, and in 1990, Sainte Famille opened its doors for the first time.

As with Jost and Grand Pré before it, Sainte Famille was faced with the fact that it takes many years to bring a vineyard into profitable production. Both Grand Pré and Jost obtained relatively large quantities of grapes

Tractor moving harvesting containers

from other sources so that they had wine to sell while they continued to develop their Nova Scotia vineyards. The operations had to become large enough to generate necessary cash flow over this long time frame.

The Sainte Famille philosophy, however, has been to stay small. Suzanne and Doug, who headed the Halifax Industrial Commission prior to his retirement, projected that their optimum size would be an annual production of 6,000 to 7,000 cases. At present, they produce about 4,000 cases. By remaining small,

the Corkums believe they have avoided the financial risks associated with growth. Even more important, by remaining small, Suzanne believes that she will be able to more quickly achieve her goal of making all the Sainte Famille wines from one hundred per cent Nova Scotia-grown grapes. At present, eighty-five per cent of the wines Sainte Famille sells are of Nova Scotia origin and many are already one hundred per cent Nova Scotia-grown, so she is, indeed, well on her way.

Suzanne and Doug Corkum

Today, Sainte Famille has thirty acres of vineyards in production, five acres devoted to red grapes and the remaining twenty-five to white varieties. The property is sixty-five acres altogether so that the winery has sufficient room for expansion to meet its planned production targets with estate-grown grapes. The winery obtains eighty-five per cent of its Nova Scotia grown grapes from its own vineyard with the remaining fifteen per cent drawn from other contract growers. Suzanne admits this could change, though, as many of the "first generation" growers were hobbyists with per-

haps only one acre or less of wine grapes. Today, more people have become interested in setting up commercially practical vineyards and there is a growing body of "know how" that they can rely on.

Suzanne Corkum believes that so much has been learned over the last few years that the future for wine growing looks exhilarating. What Nova Scotia lacked in the past was local expertise on the growing and harvesting of wine grapes. Local growers had to seek outside expertise and develop their own body of knowledge as they went along. Corkum gives a

TASTING NOTES

Sainte Famille makes a full range of table wines including the single grape whites Seyval Blanc, l'Acadie Blanc, and the German Riesling-styled Siegfried. The winery also produces reserve versions of Seyval and l'Acadie which are aged for six months in Hungarian oak. With the exception of Siegfried, the whites are very dry, suitable for pairing with seafood and white meat dishes. The remaining white, Avon Blanc, is made in an off-dry style that can be served as an aperitif or with fruit, cheese or even light desserts. The Sainte Famille Rose has proven to be popular with visitors and locals alike. It is an excellent aperitif and ideal for summer picnics and antipasto.

MARECHAL FOCH RESERVE, 2003
$19.99

Made from Old Vines Foch originally planted in 1979, this deeply concentrated red shows what a difference mature vines can make. Among the reds, the Marechal Foch undergoes partial carbonic maceration. This is similar to the technique used to enhance the fruity freshness of Beaujolais. The 2002 had a developed earthy dark plum and subtle spice on the nose which gave way to a more cherry-like sweet fruit on the palate. Flavours are rounded and the wine is well-balanced, with good weight and medium length on the well-integrated fruit, oak, and light spicy finish.

lot of credit to Andrew Jamieson, an Agriculture Canada plant breeder in Kentville, who turned his plant-breeding skills towards helping the emerging viticulture. He has hybridized numerous grape varieties over the years, seeking out characteristics that will produce the best results in Nova Scotia.

In Germany, similar research has been under way since 1945 and only now are the Germans making definitive choices. Typically, it takes at least seven years for the characteristics of such crossings to be

Stainless steel fermentation tanks

fully tested. Recent successes in Nova Scotia have even spurred inquiries from Ontario nurseries interested in propagation rights. For the time being, however, such rights will be retained here. "Nova Scotia growers," says Suzanne Corkum, "should be the main beneficiaries in the future. Our success in growing grapes has jumped dramatically in the last five years and this will be reflected in great improvements in quality and a definitive local style." There are unique advantages to build on as well. Nova Scotia growers have a more difficult time wintering their grapes, but on the other hand the cool climate produces more intense fruit. Another advantage is pest and disease resistance. Over the many years that Sainte Famille has been growing grapes, they have never had to use insecticide. As well, the need to spray against mildew is greatly reduced.

Among white varieties, Sainte Famille has had most success with the French-American hybrids, Seyval Blanc and Vidal, as well as l'Acadie Blanc. A German crossing, Siegfried, has also shown promise. Marechal Foch

TASTING NOTES

RESERVE FOCH

This recent addition to the Sainte Famille line is aged for one year in American and French oak. With its more concentrated character, it will benefit from additional bottle aging.

BACO NOIR $15.99

This is another French/American hybrid that is producing some exciting wine in Nova Scotia. Made first in the 2002 vintage, the wine was aged in French and American oak. It has a smoky, almost tar-like character on the nose, together with plenty of plum, cherry, and sweet spice. Big, generous plummy fruit, firm tannins, vibrant acidity, and hints of coffee and dark chocolate on the palate make this one a great match for a sizzling grilled steak, game dishes, or strong, hard-ripened cheese.

TASTING NOTES

SIEGFRIED, 2005 ANNAPOLIS VALLEY
$10.99

Slight smoky pungency with floral and
citrus scents, opening up in the mouth
with fresh peach flavours and gentle
acidity. Floral and honeyed notes linger
on the lightly off-dry finish.

ROSÉ, 2005 ANNAPOLIS VALLEY $10.99

Brilliant cranberry-red colour and cherry and herbal scents on the nose. Fresh
strawberry and tart cranberry flavours
are backed by brisk acidity, concluding
with a fresh, clean finish and a touch of
sweetness.

Sainte Famille wines are reasonably
priced, with the varietals selling from
$10.99- $11.99 and the Reserve range
from $12.99 up to $15.99 for the excellent Baco Noir.

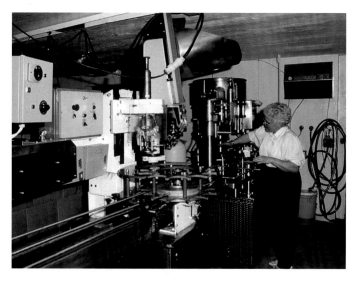

Suzanne Corkum working on the bottling machinery

appears to be the grape of choice among reds, as the
Russian variety Michurinetz has proven to be a lot more
finicky. The winery believes in the "judicious" use of
oak for white wines as well as reds. Suzanne, who has
been the winemaker as well as the owner since 1991,
feels that the climate dictates the need for a certain
amount of wood aging to soften the wines.

Hours:

April–December: Monday–Saturday 9-5;
Sunday 12-5

January-March: Monday–Saturday 9-5

Tours at 11 a.m. and 2 p.m. daily

Location: Dyke Road and Dudley Park Lane,
Falmouth (exit 7 off highway 101)

Contact: 1-800-565-0993
www.st-famille.com
scorkum@st-famille.com

Winemaker: Suzanne Corkum

LUNENBURG COUNTY WINERY
Hinterland Champion of Nova Scotia Fruit Wines

Lunenburg County established a world-class shipbuilding and fishing industry that was centred around the Grand Banks cod fishery. Much of the soil throughout the county is rich enough to support agriculture, and the industrious Lunenburg County farms produced barley, rye, oats, turnips, potatoes, and cabbage, as well as staples such as veal, lamb, butter, cheese, poultry, and beef that would be sold in Halifax. The results of this farming and fishing industry produced some unique food traditions that combined seafood and produce with old-world cooking and festive celebrations. Celebrations along the south shore meant that good food and wine were always present when festive affairs such as barn-raising days, hay-making frolics, quilting bees,

and of course weddings took place. Today, the Lunenburg County Winery continues that way of life by combining the area's rich agricultural history with its festive spirit.

About twenty-four kilometres inland from exit 11 (Blockhouse) on Highway 103 you come to the small community of Newburne, the scenic location of Lunenburg County Winery. The route along Walburne Road, following the vineyard signs, takes you through rolling hills and sparkling lakes, which seem to appear at every new bend in the road. The winery itself occupies an impressive hillside setting, with

views in every direction over the lovely and unspoiled countryside.

Winemaker Dan Sanft and his wife Heather bought the one-hundred-acre property in 1980. Here, together with Heather's father Les Southwell, they conceived the idea of establishing a small winery. The dream came to fruition when they received their commercial winery licence in 1994. Early experiments with planting vinifera grapes proved disappointing and even hybrid varieties have been difficult to grow economically. Local deer proved to be a difficult obstacle, as they are particularly fond of the tender young grape plants. While Dan

continues to work with some grape varieties, the winery's reputation rests mainly on the wide variety of fruit wines it produces. Dan takes the view that while he can grow wine grapes locally, they are unlikely to compete successfully with those grown in the world's great wine regions. Why not work with fruits that do particularly well in Nova Scotia, he reasons. For example, the farm grows a large crop of highbush blueberries, a very late-ripening species that has a good market in New England after local varieties have passed their prime. Together with patches of wild blueberries interspersed around the property, highbush blueberries also form the raw material for blueberry wine. Lunenburg County's blueberry wines have garnered an impressive number of awards in competition over the years.

Blueberry fields at Hackmatack Farms, Lunenburg County Winery

Winemaker Dan Sanft with his father-in-law, Les Southwell

Sanft's reasoning certainly has a sound basis. In recent years blueberries have started to attract favourable notice for their healthful properties. Wild blueberries, in particular, seem to have high quantities of antioxidants that counteract carcinogens, protect against heart disease, and slow the aging process. Previous studies suggesting similar effects from drinking red grape wine stimulated a huge increase in consumption worldwide. Export prospects for blueberry wine, a less perishable product with a higher added value, look promising. The farm already exports raw blueberries to markets as far away as Japan.

The winery uses all Nova Scotia-grown fruit in its wines, much of it from the farm at Newburne and an additional property in nearby Walden. Dan has also planted elderberries, a fruit long noted for producing wines similar to established grape varieties. Elderberries need plenty of water, but the farm is able to irrigate the crop using a nearby lake. The berries are thriving and provide another source of good fruit wine.

Hours:

May–October: 9-9 daily
November–April: Monday-Saturday 9-5

Location: Highway 103 to exit 11, then 24 kilometres to Newburne.

Contact: 902-644-2415
www.canada-wine.com
info@canada-wine.com

Winemaker: Dan Sanft

TASTING NOTES

LAKE ROSSIGNOL CRANBERRY $11.46

This light yellow wine is made from white cranberries which are distinctly different from the more common red. The nose shows some mineral and herbal notes with tartly crisp berry fruit flavour on the palate and a fresh, clean finish with light balancing sweetness.

PREMIUM BLUEBERRY $11.69

The Sanfts consider this their signature wine. It is rose coloured with a ripe berry scent, a minty herbal overtone and a slight suggestion of syrupy sweetness. In the mouth, though, flavour is light with a quite delicate off-dry sweetness that suits the style. Well-balanced and easy to drink, it will be agreeable to most palates.

BEAR RIVER CHERRY $11.46

Like other Lunenburg County wines, the colour is strikingly vibrant, showing some pink with a burnished background. Bouquet is quite shy with light red fruit flavours and fairly dry on the palate. Heather Sanft notes that it pairs particularly well with ham.

HONEY MOON $11.46

Honey Moon is dry mead, the ancient honey-based drink of Norsemen and Anglo-Saxons. Dan has softened its character somewhat by adding some influence of American oak. It is rich and gold coloured with dry honeycomb and grassy herbal scents. Surprisingly dry in the mouth, flavours are citrusy, finishing with a light honey overtone. Mead is not to everyone's taste, but a drink with such an ancient history is well worth trying.

CHOCKLE CAP CAYUGA 2004 $11.00
(AVAILABLE ONLY FROM THE WINERY)

An all-grape wine using Cayuga (70 per cent) blended with New York Muscat (30 per cent), that has a bouquet of attractively aromatic green apple and hints of gooseberry (which, incidentally, grow on the property). Crisp, green, fruit flavours come through on the palate, finishing with a light trace of sweetness.

SAMBUCUS $11.00
(AVAILABLE ONLY FROM THE WINERY)

Made from one hundred per cent elderberries, Sambucus remains one of my favourites among Lunenburg County's wines, perhaps because well-made elderberry wine most closely resemble the grape. Bouquet is slightly reminiscent of certain Right Bank red Bordeaux, with blackcurrant-like fruit and earthy herbal overtones. It is well-balanced, with good fruit, some complexity, and a clean and fresh finish.

DOMAINE DE GRAND PRÉ
The Dazzling Rebirth of Nova Scotia's Pioneer Winery

Historically, the Annapolis Valley has long produced the lion's share of Nova Scotia's produce. An early agricultural community grew out of the marshlands around the valley's tidal rivers after the Acadians were able to dyke and drain the marshes. The resulting rich, red soil produced some of Canada's earliest commercial crops. The fertile orchards and reclaimed fields today still produce a bounty of fresh fruit and

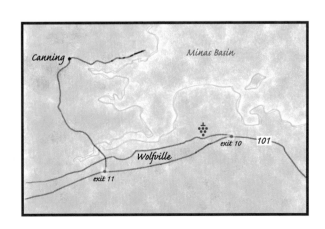

vegetables. The valley is protected from cold winds on both sides, is blessed with the most sunshine in the province, and on hot summer days, is cooled by evening breezes that blow off the Bay of Fundy to create an ideal growing climate.

It was with these advantages in hand that the new Domaine de Grand Pré opened its doors in June 2000, after five years of painstaking preparation. The winery was a huge step forward for Nova Scotia wine. When winery pioneers Roger Dial, in Grand Pré, and Hans Jost, in Malagash, brought Nova Scotia wine into being some twenty-five years ago, there were many who thought it was impossible to make quality wine in this province. The fledgling industry has experienced a bumpy road over its first quarter-century. As in all pioneering efforts, much had to be learned, as much by error as by success. The well-financed and well-researched venture of Domaine de Grand Pré, though, marked a new coming of age.

The inspiration behind Domaine de Grand Pré is Hanspeter Stutz. Hailing from Switzerland, Hanspeter is a visionary with great determination, patience, and a fierce commitment to quality. Five years is a long time to pour capital into a project without a nickel of return, but Hanspeter was determined to wait until he was absolutely ready. The results are truly impressive; Domaine de Grand Pré is, in every sense, a proud showpiece for Nova Scotia.

Founder, Hanspeter Stutz on left with son, Jurg, winemaker

The vine-covered pergola commands a magnificent view overlooking the vineyard and out to Cape Blomidon in the distance. Light summer fare is served here together, of course, with Grand Pré wines. It has also proven to be a romantic setting for wedding receptions and private parties. As many as one hundred people can be seated in the shade of the pergola. Inside, there is a fifty-seat restaurant featuring an imposing round table made from a single piece of Douglas fir. This, says Hanspeter, reflects the sociable Swiss tradition, where friends regularly gather around the table to

Elegant, abstract fountain at Domaine de Grand Pré

Jurg Stutz examines freshly-harvested grapes

share a glass of wine and chat over the day's events. In addition to wine, the restaurant offers its own cider and beer from Garrison Brewery, the Nova Scotia craft brewery, on tap. Hanspeter chose Garrison because he feels that this small brewery shares a similar philosophy: a passion to produce distinctive, high quality product on a modest scale.

Upstairs in the main winery building is an ultra-modern winebar where the Domaine's wines may be sampled. Adjoining is an elegant gift shop where the wines, as well as a range of tasteful wine-related items, may be purchased. Immediately below, with windows overlooking the action on the winery floor, is a long gallery where visitors can view rotating

TASTING NOTES

These wines can be purchased at the winery store, the Halifax Farmers' Market on Saturday mornings, and some selections may be found at NSLC outlets or at private wine stores.

L'ACADIE BLANC, 2003 $13.70

This variety makes consistently good wine here in Nova Scotia, combining lively green fruit with a steely crispness that pairs well with many local seafoods. The 2003 has ripe melon and pear scents with supple apple and pear flavours, refreshing acidity and a hint of peach on the finish.

L'ACADIE BLANC RESERVE, 2003 $16.50

Barrel aging for six months gives elegant soft fruity perfume to the bouquet, with a subtle trace of spice. Generous flavours of concentrated ripe apple are rounded out with lightly spicy, oaky vanillin. Attractive prickly acidity enlivens this polished, well-balanced wine. It has the weight to pair well with a wide variety of seafoods and white-meat dishes.

SEYVAL BLANC, 2003 $14.50

Crisply dry apple on the nose, this light, dry white has bright green apple flavours on the palate. It has a pleasing, lightly creamy texture with lively acidity and a clean fresh green fruit finish.

NEW YORK MUSCAT, 2003 $15.50

Like Sauvignon Blanc, New York Muscat is an intensely aromatic wine with a floral bouquet, slightly smoky muscat fruitiness, and a trace of peppery spice. Lusciously mouth-filling, with ripe green fruit, prickly freshness, and lingering floral and lychee flavours on the finish, it pairs especially well with spicy oriental dishes.

TASTING NOTES

LEON MILLOT, 2003 $14.50

This wine has a lively red berry on the nose, with fresh herbal and lightly spicy notes that lead into deep red fruit flavours, good tannic structure, and some earthy mineral character. It finishes long with dry fruit and dark chocolate complexity. A good match with grilled red meats, game birds, and firm-ripened cheeses.

L'ACADIE BLANC, 2005 $14.50

Nova Scotia's signature white grape combines lively green fruit with steely crisp acidity. More citrus character than usual in this vintage, with typical brisk acidity and tree fruit flavours on the finish. Pairs well with a variety of seafood and lighter dishes.

L'ACADIE BLANC RESERVE, 2005 $16.50

Oak aged six months, the bouquet displays ripe apple and a suggestion of grapefruit and light spice. Rounded citrus fruit flavours, well-balanced acidity and a mellow touch of oak on the finish impart some complexity and make for flexible pairing with seafoods and white meats.

NEW YORK MUSCAT, 2005 $16.50

An intensely aromatic floral bouquet, shows green fruit and shades of tropical fruit expanding into luscious green fruit, lychee, and grapey Muscat flavours in the mouth. Zesty crisp acidity and long floral and light tropical character reprised on the finish.

exhibitions featuring the work of various Nova Scotian artists.

The winery is also a showcase of Nova Scotia craftsmanship. Outside, the entire courtyard has been laid in cobblestones with an intricate central pattern that shows up dramatically when it rains. The stones were cut by Matthias Lange from a location near New Ross. Just below the vineyard is an abstract fountain, set in

LEON MILLOT, 2005 $14.50

Bright bitter cherry and fresh herbal notes, with bitter cherry flavours picked up on the palate along with appetizing tannic grip and correct acidity. Taste profile is quite similar to a Tuscan Sangiovese making it a natural to pair with grilled red meats, pasta, and cheese.

NEW YORK MUSCAT ICEWINE $24.50

Canadian ice wine is now widely recognized as one of the world's great dessert wines. This variety makes superb and very distinctive ice wine unique to Nova Scotia. The bouquet is extraordinarily complex, with wonderfully aromatic impressions of flowers, honey, lemon and tangerine. Elegantly refined and lusciously sweet on the palate with dynamic acid balance, its flavours are at once intense and ethereal. It finishes with rich layers of citrus fruit, floral blossoms, honey and cinnamon spice.

STUTZ HARD APPLE CIDER $10.49
(PACK OF FOUR)

Has the fragrant scent of a crisp, freshly cut apple with just a touch of sweetness in the mouth, but with balancing acidity and a refreshingly light spritz. Light-bodied, with 4.5 per cent alcohol and clean finish, it makes an ideal thirst quencher.

SEYVAL BLANC, 2005 $14.50

Like biting into a sappy green apple, with fresh crunchy tartness and a light, dry honeyed sensation through the finish. Very dry, with vibrant acidity, making a perfect match for oysters on the half shell.

the cobblestones. Floodlit at night, the water streams down basalt columns, creating a remarkable seamless effect. Ian Hope-Simpson, a blacksmith from nearby South Mountain, did the splendid wrought iron work. The site has been carefully landscaped and planted so that something will be in bloom during every season. This is the work of Avondale landscape architect Casimir Hagmann. Carpentry throughout the project

LOCAL SHRIMP WITH SPICY MELON SHOOTER

(mussels can be substituted for shrimp; serve with New York Muscat)

SHRIMP INGREDIENTS:

1 lb. peeled and de-veined
  31-40 count shrimp
2 scallions, finely sliced
1 teaspoon fresh ginger, minced
1/4 cup fresh cilantro, finely chopped
Zest and juice of one lime
1 teaspoon sesame oil

SHOOTER INGREDIENTS:

ripe melon, peeled and seeded
2 teaspoons ginger, minced
2 cloves garlic, minced
1/4 red onion, diced
1 and 1/2 cups vegetable broth
2 tablespoons rice vinegar
2 tablespoons sweet chili sauce

SHRIMP DIRECTIONS:

Combine shrimp, scallions, ginger, cilantro, lime juice and zest.

Add 1 teaspoon of sesame oil to a wok.

Place wok on medium-high heat.

When oil begins to smoke add shrimp.

Sauté until shrimp are a vibrant orange. Let cool.

SHOOTER DIRECTIONS:

Place all ingredients into a blender and purée until smooth. Refrigerate overnight.

To serve, fill shot glasses with melon shooter and rest a shrimp on side of the glass.

(Recipes created by Mark DeWolf, certified sommelier)

is the work of Bird's Eye Builders from Canning and the interior design is by Wolfville's David Ripley.

Ultimately, though, it is the wine that counts. Here, above all, there has been meticulous attention to detail and careful planning. Long before the winery reopened, Hanspeter and his son Jurg, who is the winemaker, worked with Swiss eonologist Alain Bersier to identify and develop the best vineyard sites and the most suitable grape varieties. The Stutz philosophy is to produce the highest quality wines possible from the most proven varieties. New wines will be added only if they prove viable after undergoing rigorous testing.

The wines are clean, unfaulted, and very pure renditions of the fruit. When they first came on the scene, these wines raised the benchmark for excellence. In the ensuing years, other Nova Scotia producers have risen to meet the challenge.

Hours:

May–October: 10-6 daily
April, October-December:
Wednesday–Sunday 11-5
January–March: Saturday only 11-5
Restaurant open April 1–December 31

Tours: May-October 31: 11 a.m., 3 p.m., 5 p.m. Tours of ten or more people anytime by appointment.

Location: 11611 Highway #1, Grand Pré

Contact: 1-866-GPWINES
www.grandprewines.com
mail@grandprewines.ns.ca

Winemaker: Jurg Stutz

General Manager: Hanspeter Stutz

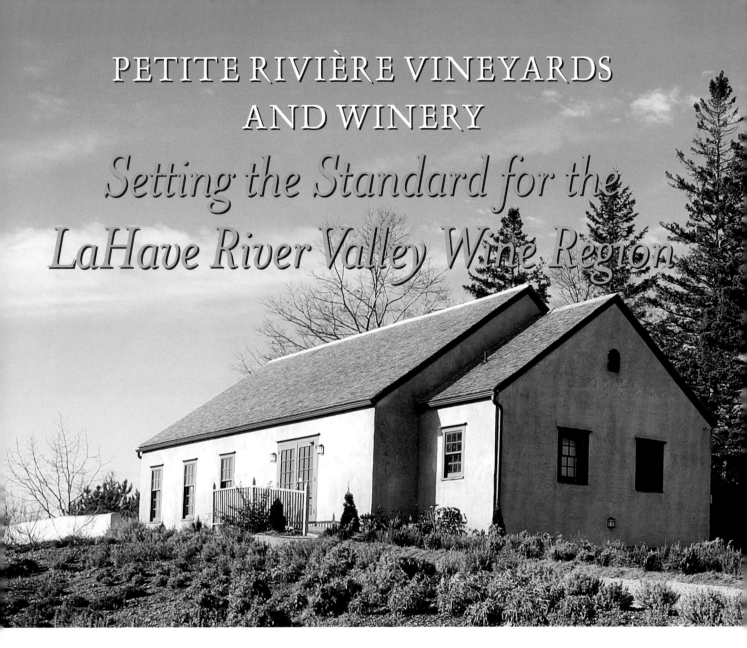

PETITE RIVIÈRE VINEYARDS AND WINERY
Setting the Standard for the LaHave River Valley Wine Region

Petite Rivière Vineyards and Winery is one of two new wineries that opened in the summer of 2004. It is located close to Crousetown in the promising LaHave River Valley wine region. Petite Rivière has two separate vineyards, St. Mary's Vineyard and Harmon's Hill. The small, welcoming winery building overlooks the more recently planted five-acre St. Mary's Vineyard, named after the nearby parish church. The seven-acre

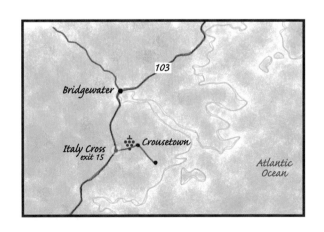

Harmon's Hill site can be seen at some distance across the rolling hills. It was first developed by owners Philip and Carol Wamboldt in 1994. Harmon's Hill is planted with hybrids, especially the red varieties such as Leon Millot and Lucy Kuhlmann. The Wamboldts believe that the St. Mary's Vineyard is more suitable for vinifera and they are growing Pinot Noir, Pinot Meunier, Chardonnay, and Zweigelt there, along with some hybrids.

Early releases included a small quantity of Chardonnay, since sold out, and four blended wines ranging in price from fourteen dollars

Carol and Philip Wamboldt with daughter, Marie Claire

TASTING NOTES

CÔTES DE LAHAVE SUR LIE, 2002 $18.00

This Seyval Blanc (80 per cent), L'Acadie Blanc (20 per cent) blend was, said Philip, inspired by Muscadet. It has spent fifteen months on the lees and, like Muscadet, has a sappy green apple character, high acidity, and bone-dry finish. It pairs quite well with oysters on the half shell.

CÔTES DE LAHAVE PREMIÈRE CUVÉE, 2002 $14.00

A blend of two hybrids, this lighter style red shows slightly shy red berry fruit on the nose with richer, black cherry and chocolate flavours on the palate. The acidity is rather high with a clean, slightly sharp finish. It is best matched with tomato-based pasta dishes and hard-ripened cheeses.

CÔTES DE LAHAVE HARMON'S HILL, 2002 $16.00

Three hybrid varieties make up this cuvée which has seen partial oak aging and chaptalization (the addition of some sugar during fermentation). Phillip felt that chaptalizing adds some smoothness and a rounder mouth feel. The bouquet has attractive cherry, dark berry, and light herbal overtones. There is good, concentrated fruit in the mouth with high acidity and a clean bitter cherry finish. It will improve with three to five years further aging.

to twenty-four dollars. Wines are available only from the winery, the Halifax Farmers' Market, and on selected local wine lists in the south shore region. The first wines released were from the difficult 2002 vintage which posed some challenges for ripening; the wines are crisp and relatively high in acidity. The 2003 vintage revealed greater roundness and ripeness. Although Philip Wamboldt began to have doubts about the economic viability of vinifera varieties in the region, other growers on the south shore are confident that classic vinifera can do well here. Look for more Chardonnay and even Pinot Noir in the next couple of years.

Shortly before Christmas 2005, Philip Wamboldt, founder and owner of the Petite Rivière winery, tragically lost his life in a highway accident. His untimely death is an enormous loss not only to his young widow Carol, co-owner of the winery, and their infant child, but also to the entire Nova Scotia wine industry. He was one of its true wine pioneers.

Until quite recently, the emergence of an exciting new region on the south shore was a well-kept secret. Philip Wamboldt was the inspiration and the driving force behind this phenomenon. He possessed a passionate attachment to the LaHave River Valley, its history, people, and soil. He quietly went about analyzing the potential for various sites in the region that might be suitable for vineyards. He came to

know the LaHave region and its various climates and soils like the back of his hand. Perhaps more than anyone else, he understood the importance of terroir, that combination of soil, climate, and topography that is so critical to success in Nova Scotia's cool-climate viticulture.

In 1992, together with his second cousin, Dr. Chris Naugler, and Dr. Bruce Wright, Philip published the *Nova Scotia Winegrower's Guide.* It was seen as quite a coup that this timely little publication, a landmark for the industry as a whole, should originate from a virtually unknown upstart region. Subsequently, south shore winegrowers were affectionately dubbed "the Bridgewater Mafia," a title they wore with some pride.

TASTING NOTES

CÔTES DE LaHAVE BARREL AGED RESERVE, 2002 $24.00

Bouquet is quite elegant, showing black-berry and dark cherry scents with subtle spicy overtones. Sweet, rich fruit and good weight on the palate lead into the well-integrated finish showing fruit, spice and subtle oak. Once again, acidity was a bit on the high side, so give it some further time in the bottle.

CÔTES DE LaHAVE BARREL AGED RESERVE, 2003 $20.00

Aging in American oak barrels for over a year has resulted in added complexity and roundness on the palate. Ripe dark fruit, fine tannins, and mellow acidity make it pleasant to drink right now. Pair with robustly flavoured meats and game dishes.

CÔTES DE LaHAVE TERRES ROCHEUX, 2003 $27.00

"Les terres rocheux," meaning the rock-iest soils, produce the best wines here. The red grapes used in this blend of Leon Millot and Lucy Kuhlmann achieved remarkable ripeness in 2003. This wine was aged in French oak barrels for one year, and shows perfumed plum and red berry scents with cedary oak and spicy notes on the nose. Plum fruit flavours are backed up with clove and cinnamon spiciness and dark chocolate richness. Youthful acidity needs a bit of time to settle down. A big, impressively concentrated wine, best with a couple of years additional aging.

Philip Wamboldt's leadership, inspiration and support extended to helping dozens of people every year in assessing the potential of their property for growing vines. He was also generous with his vineyard equipment, loaning it out freely to other growers throughout the year. Carol Wamboldt continues oper-ating the winery with the assistance of Niagara College-trained Ben Sweatenham. Some wines from the 2005 vintage were released in spring 2006, and several reds from earlier vintages will also be ready for release this year.

TASTING NOTES

CÔTES DE LAHAVE SUR LIE, 2003 $17.00

"Sur Lie" means aged on the "lees," the residue left after fermentation. It adds an attractive yeasty, baked bread character. This wine has crisp green apple aromas and generous ripe apple flavour. It matches well with fresh, simple prepared seafood.

BEAR HILLS CHARDONNAY, 2004 $20.00

Grown at the Bear Hills Vineyard in Upper LaHave where Chardonnay manages to thrive, this is a crisp, unoaked style reminiscent of Chablis. It shows ripe apple and pear character and will pair well with most fish and white-meat dishes.

CÔTES DE LAHAVE ROSÉ, 2005 $12.00

A vibrantly aromatic dry rosé with the inviting scent of fresh raspberries. Crisp acidity makes for refreshing summer drinking. Best served lightly chilled with light picnic foods.

Hours: Thursday-Sunday: 12-5.

Tours by appointment.

Location: 1300 Italy Cross Road, Crousetown (exit 15 on highway 103)

Contact: 902-693-3033
cslack@eastlink.ca

Winemaker: Carol Slack-Wamboldt

Salmon and Dill Pancakes

(serve with L'Acadie Blanc)

1 large salmon fillet (8-10 oz.)

3 teaspoons lemon zest

2 eggs, lightly beaten

1 cup all-purpose flour

1 8 oz. container plain yogurt, divided

1/2 cup finely chopped chives

1 cup finely chopped green onions

soya or other lightly flavoured oil

1/4 cup freshly chopped dill

Juice of 1/2 a lemon

Remove skin from salmon. Chop salmon into small chunks. Place salmon in bowl and refrigerate until ready. Add zest, eggs, flour, and 2 tablespoons of yogurt to a bowl and beat/whisk until smooth. Mix in chives, green onions, and salmon to mixture and mix until well incorporated. Heat a large frying pan over medium heat, adding 1-2 tablespoons of oil. Place tablespoon of mixture in pan, pressed down with ladle to form pancake and cook until golden brown on each side. Add more pancakes, and repeat until all are cooked. Remove pancakes from pan and place on paper towel. Add dill, juice of half a lemon and yogurt to a bowl and mix thoroughly. To serve, reheat pancakes, add teaspoon of yogurt dill sauce and garnish with a sprig of dill.

GASPEREAU VINEYARDS
Picturesque Setting and Persuasive Wines

In the summer of 2004, Nova Scotia added two new licensed wineries, Petite Rivière Vineyards and Winery in the south shore region, and Gaspereau Vineyards in the picturesque Gaspereau Valley.

The Gaspereau property is owned by Hans Christian Jost and his wife Karen of the Malagash-based Jost Vineyards, the largest and longest-established operation in the province. The new winery, though, has its own identity

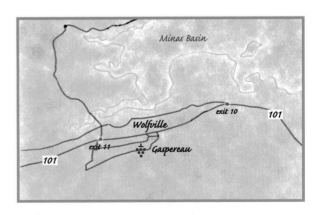

and a complete range of wines under the Gaspereau Vineyards label. Other than Jost, most successful vineyards in Nova Scotia were initially established in the nearby Annapolis Valley, and winemakers have long understood that the smaller and more sheltered Gaspereau Valley offers some unique advantages for grape growing. Gaspereau's vineyard is a perfect example, occupying an ideal south-facing slope overlooking the river. It is snugly sheltered from cold northerly and north-westerly winds and gets plenty of exposure to the sun. Except in the lowest corner of the vineyard, the angle of slope also protects against the danger of killing frosts. These conditions make for a

longer growing season and higher quality grapes. The site covers some sixty-seven acres, of which thirty-five acres have been planted with vines; thirty acres are now producing quality fruit. Most heavily planted are French-American hybrids, proven varieties that thrive in Nova Scotia's cool-climate conditions. They include the whites, L'Acadie Blanc, New York Muscat, Vidal, and Seyval Blanc along with the reds, Lucy Kuhlmann (an earlier ripening variation similar to Marechal Foch) and De Chaunac.

Some prime acreage on the site has been planted with viniferas including Chardonnay, Riesling, Cabernet Franc, Pinot Noir, and the

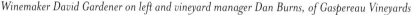

Winemaker David Gardener on left and vineyard manager Dan Burns, of Gaspereau Vineyards

TASTING NOTES

NEW YORK MUSCAT BENJAMIN BRIDGE, 2003 $13.95

Grapes for this wine come from the Benjamin Bridge vineyard, also in the Gaspereau Valley, and were hand-harvested and crushed within minutes of picking. The wine has lovely floral, musky, and spicy aromatics and mellow mouth-filling fresh green fruit flavours. It finishes with green fruit and lychee notes and lingering floral character. It makes an interesting contrast with the same grape variety, New York Muscat, listed below.

DE CHAUNAC, 2003 $14.95

The bouquet is full of cool-climate bright cherry and herbal green pepper scents. Black cherry flavour in the mouth is packaged in a thick, velvety texture with some dark chocolate and herbal over-tones and a long, dark fruit finish. It has good structure and is worth laying down for a couple of years when it will shed some youthful acidity.

LUCY KUHLMANN, 2003 $19.99

Complex developed plum and dark berry fruit with cedary spice on the nose. Good depth of fruit and firm but agreeable tannins in the mouth. Youthful acidity will mellow out over the next couple of years. The prolonged finish has well-integrated fruit, spice and judicious supporting oak.

NEW YORK MUSCAT, 2005 $14.99

Remarkable pungent bouquet with smoky Muscat intensity, lychee and floral blossoms. Classic Nova Scotia Muscat flavours show zesty green fruit, lychee, and spicy peppery notes. Good weight in the mouth and a long, floral aromatic and crisp fresh fruit finish.

L'ACADIE BLANC, 2005 $12.99

Unusually lush for l'Acadie, with ripe tropical fruit, citrus and melon bouquet and equally remarkable ripe pink grapefruit, melon, and even some pineapple on the palate and long fruity intensity on the finish. A terrific wine for the money and a new dimension for l'Acadie Blanc.

The Warner Vineyard, Centreville, Nova Scotia

TASTING NOTES:

LUCY KUHLMANN, 2001 $18.95

Quite developed on the nose with evolved fruit, cedary spice, and lightly gamey overtones, this wine has dark cherry and rich chocolate flavours, with firm tannins and plenty of acidity. The well-integrated finish shows dark fruit, vanillin, and lingering cedary oak. Drinking quite well now, but will be better with another three to four years in the cellar.

L'ACADIE BLANC, 2003 $14.95

Intensely aromatic, with intriguing notes of grapefruit and green apple, this wine delivers concentrated green apple flavour with some lychee overtones on the palate. It finishes with zesty acidity and crisp fresh peach.

NEW YORK MUSCAT, 2003 $17.95

Grapes for this wine come from the Gaspereau vineyard and the Warner vineyard in the Annapolis Valley. It shows plenty of floral perfume with some spice and a hint of white pepper. Green fruit and distinctive, grapey Muscat flavours fill the mouth. There is good weight and acidity and a lingering, spicy aromatic finish.

Austrian cross, Zweigelt. Conventional wisdom has it that viniferas are not hardy enough to survive our harsh winter conditions. Promising early results in Gaspereau, though, as well as in some other vineyards around Nova Scotia, give cause for cautious optimism.

The winery occupies a trim new building, very much in harmony with the local surroundings. There is a tasting bar and shop where you can purchase Gaspereau Vineyard wines as well as other specialty items. Although there is no restaurant, picnic tables are provided and visitors are welcome to bring their own food. The Gaspereau Valley makes a beautiful setting for the new winery and the easy one-hour drive from Halifax makes it a pleasant afternoon jaunt. If you can't make it to the winery, Gaspereau Vineyard wines are also available at the Bishop's Cellar, Premier Wine and Spirits in Dartmouth, and VinArt in Bayers Lake.

Hours: May–December: 9-6

Tours: 12 p.m., 2 p.m., 4 p.m.

Location: 2239 White Rock Road, Gaspereau
From highway 101, take exit 11 and follow the vineyard signs seven kilometres to Gaspereau. From Wolfville, take Gaspereau Avenue and follow it for three kilometres.

Contact: 902-542-1455
www.gaspereauwine.com
info@gaspereauwine.com

Vineyard Manager: Dan Burns

Winemaker: David Gardener

Manager: Kim Strickland

BEAR RIVER VINEYARDS
Emerging New Wine Region

Tucked away in the more temperate southwest corner of Nova Scotia lies the picturesque and largely fog-free Bear River. The river valley is similar to that other emergent wine valley, the Gaspereau, and both bear a certain resemblance to Germany's Mosel Valley. All three are relatively steep and narrow valleys with winding rivers that create a series of south-facing slopes. In northerly climates these sheltered and sunny locations provide particularly favourable conditions for viticulture.

Perhaps because Bear River is so far removed from the more established Nova Scotia wine country, very few people know that Chris Hawes has been quietly growing grapes in this

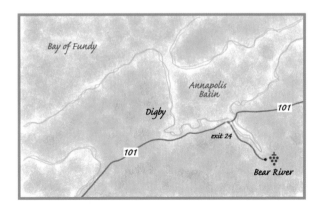

previously overlooked part of Nova Scotia. It is quite a thrill to discover this scenic and, by now, well-established vineyard. Early this year, Hawes, who caught the wine bug when working in the Niagara vineyards as a teenager, finally obtained a license to open a winery. The winery occupies a well-preserved former barn and the vineyard below sweeps down a well-drained, southwest-facing slope towards the river. Even more surprising is the fact that many of the grapes thriving in this small vineyard are classic viniferas such as Chardonnay, Pinot Noir,

Riesling, and Auxerrois. These tender European varieties have done remarkably well in this relatively benign setting, having survived through several harsh winters. Although many veteran Nova Scotia grapegrowers remain skeptical about the viability of viniferas in this region, Hawes states confidently, "Any vine on

TASTING NOTES

I have tasted three Bear River wines from the soon-to-be-released first vintage, 2005. Pricing details are not yet available.

RIESLING, 2005

Very pale-green colour with fresh green fruit and grassy herbal scents and a hint of apricot on the nose. Very clean, fresh green apple flavours on the palate and crunchy white peach on the finish. Acidity, though, is aggressive and needs some toning down. Potential is clearly evident and will likely be fully realized in future vintages.

CHARDONNAY, 2005

Intensely aromatic bouquet showing vibrant cool-climate expression of grapefruit and crisp peach with more green apple character and zesty acidity on the palate. The chameleon grape, Chardonnay takes on an intriguing new identity with very pure aromatic and crisp green fruit personality. This is the most balanced of the three.

PINOT NOIR, 2005

The wine is unfiltered and somewhat cloudy in the glass. Colour is more akin to a light rose than a true red. Bouquet has charming fresh strawberry perfume, authentically Pinot Noir in character. True Pinot flavour shows up on the palate with some savoury and peppery notes. Once again, acidity is problematic. If this can be managed successfully in future vintages it will be convincing evidence that good Pinot can be made in Bear River.

Chris Hawes and wife, Peggy

this site that made it into its third year, will make it into its hundredth."

With the emergence of Nova Scotia's "newest" wine regions, the south shore and now Bear River, Nova Scotia viticulture appears to have come full circle. As noted in the introduction, we know that Isaac de Razilly planted grapes on the LaHave in the 1630s and there is persuasive evidence that a vineyard was planted in Bear River as early as 1611, making it the first in Nova Scotia. The French obviously knew a thing or two about vines and chose their vineyard sites carefully. Modern climatology has confirmed that Bear River is milder than the Annapolis Valley and that the LaHave River Valley enjoys a similar advantage. Now that grape growing is well and truly

established in the Annapolis Valley, it is exciting to imagine what can be accomplished in these new settings, where conditions may prove even more advantageous.

Bear River Vineyards will not have an on-site winery store immediately, although a visitors' centre is planned. In the meantime, visitors are always welcome. Chris Hawes plans to release his first wines for sale in September 2006. Quantities will be very small and he expects to be able to sell all he has available in locations such as the Halifax and Annapolis Royal Farmers' Markets and to select restaurants. The first offerings will include a blend of the red hybrids Baco Noir and Marechal Foch. The other releases are the single grape varietals Riesling, Chardonnay, Pinot Grigio (Pinot Gris), and Pinot Noir.

Chris Hawes has four acres under vine, three of which are now producing mature fruit. He recently acquired an adjacent plot of cleared land which provides another eight acres of vineyard potential. Chris says there are now four growers in the Bear River region and extensive new plantings will go in this year. One grower planted for the first time in 2005 and is putting in another three acres in 2006. Another, on the south side of the river, has seven acres also ready for planting. Bear River Vineyards will provide 15,000 cuttings to other growers in 2006. It appears quite likely that the region will have thirty acres or more under vine within the next couple of years. Within the foreseeable future, this lovely valley could be studded with new vines.

Hours: by appointment only.

Location: 133 Chute Road, Bear River

Contact: 902-467-4156
www.wine.travel
chris@wine.travel

Winemaker: Chris Hawes

BLOMIDON ESTATE WINERY
"Canada's Only Tidal Winery"

Blomidon Estate Winery, formerly known as Habitant, has had its ups and downs over the years, but now appears to be headed in the right direction. The vineyard lies on a very gentle, south-facing slope running down to the shore of the Minas Basin, a sheltered offshoot of the Bay of Fundy. The vineyard's close proximity to salt water, which never freezes, greatly moderates winter conditions. Consequently, frost damage is less of a hazard here than in many other locations. At present, some seventeen acres of vines are planted including both vinifera and hybrid varieties.

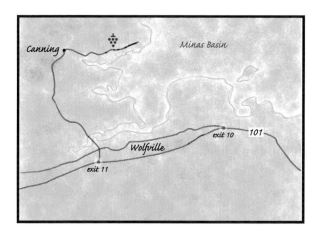

Blomidon Estate owns an additional thirty-acre vineyard at nearby Perreau Creek. Nestled in the shelter of the South Mountain with

Wes Lowrey, winemaker and winery manager, Blomidon Estate

Tourism and an Ontario wine industry veteran, joined Creekside Estate Winery as president. His arrival, along with the addition of the Mike Weir Estate Winery—a partnership between Creekside's directors and acclaimed Canadian golf professional and wine enthusiast Mike Weir—heralds a new phase of expansion. This winery, also in Niagara, is slated to open by summer 2006. Commendably, proceeds from wine sales will go to Mike Weir's charitable foundation, which supports needy children. Together with the Jensens, Barry Katzman has taken a direct interest in developments at Blomidon Estate. The new dynamism and experience in Creekside's management bodes well for the future of all three wineries.

good southerly exposure and an angle of slope that helps to shed frost, it, too, is an ideal location for growing vines. The site is currently grown over, but future redevelopment is planned. Blomidon Estate is owned by Laura McCain-Jensen and husband, Peter Jensen, who also established the Creekside Estate Winery in Niagara. Creekside's experienced winemaking team of Rob Power, a graduate of Brock University's Cool Climate Oenology and Viticulture Institute, and veteran Australian winemaker Craig McDonald, also represents a valuable resource to Blomidon Estate.

In 2005, Barry Katzman, a director of the Wine Council of Ontario, Chair of Winery

Currently, Blomidon Estate wines are made by Wes Lowrey, who also manages the property. Wes comes from the Niagara region, where his family are growers who supply grapes to Creekside. He completed a master's degree at Brock University and a winemaking course, both while continuing to work part-time at the Creekside winery. Wes first came to Nova Scotia to help with the 2002 harvest and made the move permanent the following year. He is a firm believer in the future of Nova Scotia wine. "We have," he says, "the opportunity to do things the right way from early on." In the case of Blomidon Estate, this means remaining small

TASTING NOTES

BARREL FERMENTED CHARDONNAY, 2003 $18.95

Crisp fresh green fruit on the nose is softened by vanilla spice and light traces of oak. Plenty of green apple comes through on the palate with a clean, fresh finish and just a hint of butter. Light and appealing and an excellent match with local seafoods.

BACO NOIR, 2003 $13.99

Youthful purple with an elegant plum and black cherry bouquet backed by spicy oak and light, leafy herbal notes. Black cherry and peppery spice flavours offer future promise. Acids need time to soften.

and working with high-quality, local fruit. "We must," says Wes, "go the 100% Nova Scotia route." The 2004 harvest was entirely estate-grown and will yield some 1,500 cases. The goal is to produce 5,000 cases per annum, and possibly more if high-quality, local grapes can be obtained from local contract growers.

Blomidon has had some success with vinifera varieties as well as the more prevalent hybrids. Both Chardonnay and Pinot Noir were planted several years ago, and more recently, five hundred Shiraz vines were planted on a trial basis. Surprisingly, 75% of these tender young vines survived temperatures as low as -18 degrees Celsius. Pinot Noir, however, has not fared as well and has been replaced with the sturdier hybrid, Baco Noir. Baco has shown the most promise among the reds and there are seven acres of this variety planted on site. Whites make up the rest of the vineyard with four acres of Chardonnay and three each of the hybrids, l'Acadie and Seyval.

Hours: May–September: 10-5 Monday–Friday; 12-5 Saturday and Sunday
November–April: 12-5 Saturday and Sunday only

Location: 10318 Hwy. 221, Canning

Contact: 1-877-582-7565
www.blomidonwine.com
retail@blomidonwine.com

Winemaker/Winery Manager: Wes Lowrey

ROSSIGNOL ESTATE
Prince Edward Island's Unique Winery

The eastern end of "The Island," as Maritimers familiarly call Prince Edward Island, is linked to Nova Scotia by a car ferry (capacity: 220) that runs from Caribou, Nova Scotia, near Pictou, to Wood Islands. The twenty-four kilometre crossing takes approximately one hour, fifteen minutes. It is a lovely trip and a relaxing way to arrive. About nine kilometres from the Wood Islands Ferry Terminal, at Little Sands, on the road to Murray

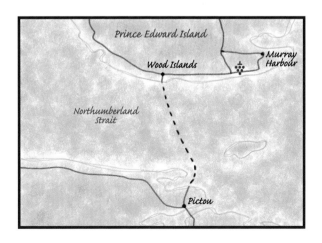

Harbour, is the picture postcard Rossignol Estate Winery. The winery occupies a spectacular setting overlooking a gentle south-facing slope sweeping down to the Northumberland Strait. Pictou Island is in the foreground and Nova Scotia can be seen in the distance.

The winery is the creation of John Rossignol, originally from Ontario. In his former life, John was a contractor working with food and beverage-processing equipment. This experience proved to be useful in setting up a winery. He is also a sailor and built his own forty-foot ketch. It was this interest in sailing that first drew him to this part of the world. In fact, he once sailed a boat from Ontario down the St. Lawrence River to Prince Edward Island. Also a talented artist, John's own paintings grace the labels of several of his wines.

A large proportion of the winery's production is made up of wines utilizing local fruit. John Rossignol believes that high quality fruit wines can match grape wines and have their place complementing fine food. The on-site winery shop has a tasting bar where the estate wines can be sampled and also purchased. The shop also serves as a showcase for local arts and crafts.

Rossignol now has seven acres in production, with another vineyard set to come on stream in the next couple of years. The plantings are French/American hybrids that thrive in local conditions. Rossignol's most interesting experiment, however, was to grow the more tender vinifera vines in greenhouses. A few years ago the Prince Edward Island tobacco industry became defunct, making greenhouse

End of the harvest—John Rossignol, Rossignol Estate

TASTING NOTES

PREMIUM OAK AGED ROSSIGNOL ISLE ST. JEAN $24.00
(ONLY AVAILABLE AT THE WINERY)

The wine shows well-developed dark berry fruit with quite elegant vanillin oak on the nose and richly concentrated blackberry-like flavours, moderate tannins and mellow rounded oak with light spice on the finish. I quite liked it, but could not identify the blend. This is, in fact, John Rossignol's "forbidden marriage between grape and fruit," an equal blend of blueberries with the hybrid grape, Marechal Foch. This non-vintage release was some three years in the making, and production was just one hundred cases in all.

ROSSIGNOL STRAWBERRY $13.50

A medium-dry rose style that the winemaker recommends as an aperitif or an accompaniment to cheese.

ROSSIGNOL RASPBERRY $13.95

This wine will appeal to those who like the intense, concentrated flavour of this fruit, which certainly comes across in the wine. It is quite sweet and can be drunk on its own or with dessert. It is also available in Nova Scotia at the Port of Wines.

ROSSIGNOL STRAWBERRY RHUBARB $14.90

This wine is aged for one year and finishes very sweet. Amber coloured, the wine shows some complexity; the tartness of rhubarb provides a good counterpoise to strawberry sweetness.

space available. Rossignol planted the equivalent of two acres of vines under glass. Viniferas such as Chardonnay, Cabernet Franc, and Pinot Noir were intensively cultivated, and initially yielded much higher quantities than the open-air vineyards. Unfortunately, he discovered that extreme temperature fluctuations caused the vines too much stress and the experiment has been discontinued.

Rossignol wines have done very well in competition, earning acclaim for both grape and fruit varieties. The winery makes some of the best fruit wines I have tasted. They are very clean and evoke the authentic appeal of fresh fruit.

Hours:
May–October: Monday–Saturday 10-5, Sunday 1-5
Winter: open by chance or call ahead.

Location: RR#4, Murray River, PE

Contact: 902-962-4193
www.rossignolwinery.com

Local cranberries ready to be crushed

Tasting Notes

Rossignol Cranberry $14.90

Made from a combination of wild and cultivated cranberries, the winery handles this wine in much the same way as a red grape. With an attractive "partridge eye" colour in the glass, it has a clean, subtle cranberry scent with a hint of astringency. On the palate there is just enough sweetness to balance the natural tartness of the berry.

Blackberry Mead $16.90

The base for this extraordinary drop is seventy-five per cent honey, so it is accurately described as mead. Blackberries, though, add complexity and fruity appeal to the finished product. It resembles a good light port, but with elegant berry fruit and subtle honeyed overtones.

Rossignol Seyval Blanc $13.10

This white is made in an off-dry style that makes it particularly suitable as an aperitif. Fruit is fresh and clean, with well-balanced acidity and a light clean finish.

Ortega Chardonnay $14.90

This oak-influenced white weighs in with 13 per cent alcohol and shows hints of vanillin together with light fruit on the nose. Full-bodied and full-flavoured, it matches well with local lobster and drawn butter.

Ragout of Rossignol
Blueberry Wine-Scented Beef

2 lbs. beef cut in 2 cm. cubes
(sirloin or flank works well)
1 1/2 cups Rossignol blueberry wine
1 1/2 tbsp. cognac
1 bouquet garni
1/2 tbs. green peppercorns
2 tbsp. vegetable oil
1/4 cup flour
1/4 tsp. crushed black pepper
1 tsp. salt
3 onions, peeled and sliced
2 large carrots, peeled and diced
1/4 lb. sliced bacon
2 tbsp. unsalted butter
1 clove garlic
15 small pearl onions
1 tsp. sugar

Marinade beef in a mixture of blueberry wine, cognac, bouquet garni, and half the peppercorns as well as half the oil for at least two hours.

Cut the bacon into 1/4-inch pieces. Parcook in a preheated frying pan, remove from heat and dry with a paper towel. Reserve. Remove the beef from the marinade. Reserve the liquid.

Melt 2 tbsp. butter with remaining oil in a large pot or Dutch oven. Lightly toss the beef in the flour, then add to the pot and sauté until tender—return the meat and bacon to the pan—add the marinade and the bouquet garni. Bring to a boil, add the garlic clove, which should be lightly crushed. Cover the pot and simmer over low heat for 2 1/2 hours.

Peel the pearl onions and add to the pot. Let simmer again until onions are tender. Serve with sautéed noodles or garlic-mashed potatoes.

Other Sites of Interest

Glenora—North America's Only Malt Whisky Distillery

Cape Breton Island, with its stunning vistas and unforgettable Cabot Trail, is a diverse region of towering cliffs and spectacular coastline alongside pleasant river valleys and green rolling hills. Large numbers of Scottish highland immigrants settled the island during the late nineteenth and early twentieth centuries and as a result, Gaelic traditions are still very alive in Cape Breton today. Besides Gaelic, English, French, and Mi'kmaq are spoken throughout the island and Celtic music and folklore traditions are vibrant expressions of the island's rich and varied culture. Ceilidh celebrations, barn dances,

TASTING NOTES

TEN-YEAR-OLD

Bouquet of dried fruit with some orangey and nutty scents and a suggestion of ginger and floral notes. Quite rich and sweet on the palate with attractively light smoky and peaty notes, dried fruit and finishing with elegant oak and spice. A big step up from the previous releases which closely resembled some Lowland Scottish styles. This one definitely has arrived, with rounder, fuller flavours, more body and more complex character than its predecessors.

FOURTEEN-YEAR-OLD

Extraordinary complexity on the nose with subtle sweet dried fruit, ginger, all-spice and dry oaky overtones. Intense, powerful, and elegant on the palate with very smooth peaty notes, orange peel, and dried fruit. Very long, smoky dry oak on the finish. A richly complex, big league whisky.

FIFTEEN-YEAR-OLD

Plenty of complexity in the bouquet showing ginger, all-spice, a trace of cinnamon spicy and orangey dried fruit with subtle floral notes and some oaky astringency. Incredibly smooth on the palate, with lovely fruity sweetness, gingery spice, rich nutty character, and lots of dry peaty smoke and oak on the finish. Lighter and more elegant on the palate than the fourteen-year-old, but the fourteen definitely has more power and richness.

kitchen parties, and church suppers are alive and well on Cape Breton as the love of music and storytelling dominates the island's way of life. The island is a pleasure to explore by foot, automobile, or boat whether off-shore or on the magnificent salt-water Bras d'Or Lakes. This inland sea supports agriculture along its coast while the lake is home to many aquaculture operations that harvest mussels, oysters, and steelhead. Food traditions of the island emphasize simple, fresh ingredients that are available locally such as fish, vegetables, and game including rabbit, deer and moose. Scottish fare includes Scotch barley broth since many of the early Scottish settlers to the island claimed to have received their brawn from being raised on broth. In early times, oatmeal was used as a thickening agent, but this gave way to barley. Soups and chowders are closely associated with the Scottish cookery traditions of Cape Breton. Haggis is the national dish of the Scots and is still consumed on the island in celebration of Robbie Burns Day along with a dram of Scotch or Cape Breton's very own Glenora malt whisky. Another interesting dish with curious origins is Cape Breton pork pies. In her classic Nova Scotia cookbook, *Out of Old Nova Scotia Kitchens*, Marie Nightingale writes: "How these little tarts got their name remains a mystery to us. It could be that pork fat was once used as the shortening, or it might just be a reflection of the wonderful Cape Breton sense of humour."

Like the scenery of Cape Breton, the cuisine is also rich and diverse. From salt cod, salmon and halibut, to lobster, oysters, and snow crab; from lamb and chicken to strawberries, blueberries, cranberries, and maple sugar, the delicacies of the island can be combined in numerous ways to create a unique and authentic tasting experience.

Nestled in this unique land is the singular Glenora Distillery. North America's only malt whisky distillery is superbly set in a beautiful valley surrounded by the spectacular Mabou Highlands. The building closely resembles the design of classic malt distilleries in the Scottish Highlands. It is only fitting that this distillery be located here. Along the western coast of Cape Breton, the ancestral Gaelic culture is very much alive and Glenora embodies that tradition.

Originally the dream of a local visionary, the late Bruce Jardine, today's impressive showpiece has been a long time in the making. As malt whisky aficionados will know, it takes time for this spirit to achieve proper maturity, typically a minimum of eight to ten years. Building a distillery from scratch is an expensive proposition and ten years is a long time to wait before seeing any return on investment. Not surprisingly, the road has been difficult and Bruce Jardine, unfortunately, did not live to see his vision completely fulfilled. Current owners Lauchie MacLean and Bob Scott,

TASTING NOTES

Apparently, the distinctive character of the fourteen-year-old comes from the unusual barrel-aging process. First aged in bourbon cask, it then spent some time in rum and sherry casks before being returned to bourbon cask for finishing. Only 120 bottles of this extraordinary whisky were made. Unfortunately, these are virtually all gone.

Glen Breton Rare ten-year-old is currently available at the Nova Scotia Liquor Corporation's Port of Wines, priced at $79.99. It is not inexpensive, but this really is a rare spirit, Nova Scotia's unique entry in the world of fine whisky.

Maclellan's Brook

imported—the barley from Scotland, and the yeast from South Africa. Scottish barley, says Bob Scott, is more effective than Canadian varieties in producing the necessary level of alcohol during fermentation. South African yeast, derived from molasses, also boosts alcohol and is, in fact, used by most Scottish distilleries.

Glenora's single malt, Glen Breton Rare, is lightly peated and aging takes place in used bourbon casks from Kentucky and Tennessee. Initial releases did not carry an age statement, but the first, says Bob, was an eight-year-old, followed last year with a nine-year-old. The current release has been aged for ten years. Glenora has also made limited quantities of older whiskies including a fourteen-year-old and a fifteen-year-old.

though, share his commitment and are passionately focused on making great malt whisky.

The site was chosen not for its spectacular beauty, but rather for the source of pure water provided by Maclellan's Brook. The brook, which runs right beside the distillery, is fed by twenty-two natural mountain streams flowing through the surrounding highlands. It supplies the one-million-litre holding pond from which the water is drawn. Pure water is essential to making good whisky and Glenora has acquired six hundred acres of surrounding land in order to protect this critical supply. The other ingredients, barley and yeast, are

Hours: Glenora offers regularly scheduled distillery tours during the season which runs from May 16 to October 16

Other Distillery Features: There is a welcoming inn with nine rooms and a fine restaurant and pub which has live Gaelic entertainment including local fiddlers and step dancers. Visitors can also stay at one of four picturesque hillside chalets which boast breathtaking views over the valley.

Craft Breweries and Brew Pubs

Drawing off a fresh pint at the Propeller Brewery

The Halifax metropolitan area of Nova Scotia (now called the Halifax Regional Municipality, or HRM) is an eclectic mix of historic architecture and modern skyscrapers. The centre of the city is a fascinating collection of historical landmarks, boutiques, cafés, restaurants, and favourite old watering holes. Brew pubs and craft breweries are notable local attractions. The city's waterfront from Historic Properties to Pier 21 has been extensively redeveloped and the old port city now boasts an impressive bustling harbour that houses extensive cargo and cruise ship traffic. This is a city of public parks with the Halifax Public Gardens and Point Pleasant Park most impressive when in full bloom. From the vantage point on Citadel Hill, the old fortress still offers the most impressive views of the second-largest natural harbour in the world. The Farmers' Market dates back to the founding of Halifax in the early 1750s when most Haligonians would include a regular trip to the

Rogues Roost, home to some of Nova Scotia's finest craft beers

province including at Preston, outside Dartmouth, where an escaped American slave, William Deer, established a restaurant and inn in the nineteenth century known as Deer's Castle. The inn soon became famous and in 1859, Frederick Cozzins wrote a description of the place in his book, *Acadia, or a Month with the Blue Noses*: "William Deer, who lives here, keeps the best wine and beer, bandy, and cider, and other good cheer. Fish and ducks, and moose and deer, caught or shot in the woods near here with cutlets or steaks, as will appear; If you will stop you will need not fear. But you will be well treated by William Deer, and by Mrs. Deer, his dearest, deary dear!"

The Irish settled around Nova Scotia but their influence throughout HRM has been extensive, especially with regard to food and cookery. Traditional Nova Scotian Irish stew includes mutton and potatoes layered with onions and cooked in a stewpot. According to Marie Nightingale, proper Irish stew means the pot must be shaken while cooking rather than stirred. Irish potato biscuits and Irish potato cakes are also popular traditional fare eaten by the Irish at breakfast and according to Nightingale, the secret to success "depends upon the softness of the dough, light handling and quick baking."

market at Cheapside every Saturday morning. Indeed, Cheapside was an appropriate name, for when Charles Dickens first visited the market in 1849 he reported that the site was "abundantly supplied and exceedingly cheap."

HRM is the most cosmopolitan region of Nova Scotia and many ethnic communities have established vibrant cultures as well as interesting culinary traditions. German, Dutch, English, French, Irish, and Scottish immigrants came to Halifax and more recently Greek, Italian, Middle Eastern, and Asian immigrants have settled around the Halifax Regional Municipality. To recognize this diversity, a multicultural festival is held every summer on the Dartmouth waterfront showcasing cuisine from around the world. Numerous blacks arrived in Halifax prior to the American Revolution, many as free Loyalists, but other as slaves. They established communities in many parts of the

Garrison Brewing's new location at historic Pier 21.

Since Halifax experienced numerous waves of immigrants that were often down on their luck, the public soup house became an institution in the nineteenth century, distributing a hearty dish called "charitable soup" or the "soup for the poor." During the spring of 1818, one hundred gallons of soup were made from beef and vegetables and fed to the poor immigrants from Europe. Like the city itself, the cuisine of Halifax is plentiful and varied, drawn from customs and culinary traditions from around the globe. It is in this eclectic atmosphere that one will find some of Nova Scotia's finest craft breweries and brew pubs, including the Garrison and Propellor breweries and Rogue's Roost.

Even for a wine enthusiast there is something special about the incomparable aroma of fresh malt, hops, water, and yeast doing what they do so well together—making great beer. This is not the inoffensive commercial stuff that has dominated the Canadian market for so long, but brew that is muscular, flavourful, assertive and, above all, interesting.

Granite Brewery

It is popular wisdom in the brewing business that the public cannot taste the difference between one beer and another and do not want anything with a distinctive flavour. Large commercial breweries spend fortunes promoting brands with distinctive labels rather than distinctive tastes. They may have been right about the majority of consumers, but more and more people seem to be looking for something different. These consumers are finding it from a growing group of small brewers who are dedicated to producing for others the kind of beer they themselves enjoy.

Canadians have long made fun of American beer for being watery and low in alcohol content. This may have been true when mass market products were the only available choice on either side of the border. Perhaps that is why

Americans were the first to revolt. Beginning in the western states, small breweries sprang up, making beer that awakened long dormant taste buds. In a few short years, North America has gone from a market dominated by bland, mass-market brands to one of the most dynamic and exciting markets in the world. Today, there are hundreds of small breweries making every conceivable variety of beer and having fun doing it.

In Canada, the first "brew pubs," small operations that brew fresh (unpasteurized) beer sold on the premises, opened in British Columbia. The first, in 1983, was Horseshoe Bay Brewing near Vancouver. "Microbreweries," which make similarly unique beers in small quantities for sale in bottles, quickly followed. Meanwhile, here on the east coast, Kevin Keefe had been reading about these developments and decided he wanted to do the same in Nova Scotia. First, he took a brewing course in Albany, New York, and subsequently travelled to England for three months to learn the art first-hand in a brewery and to obtain the necessary brewing equipment. The apparatus arrived in Halifax in January 1985, and Ginger's, the first brew pub east of the Rockies, opened its doors on Hollis Street in April of the same year.

Keefe's successful operation eventually moved to the historic Henry House on Barrington Street, under a new name, The Granite Brewery, which quickly became a Halifax institution. This fine old stone building is an ideal setting for enjoying real British style beers, together with good food and convivial

company. Some years ago, Keefe moved the brewery to a new location on Barrington Street where it still operates under the Granite name. Under new ownership, the original building has reverted back to being called the Henry House. Other than the location, little else has changed, as Keefe continues to do the brewing using only natural ingredients: malt, hops, water, and yeast. His beers are unfiltered to preserve maximum flavour and body. The Granite's draught beers are the English-style Best Bitter and Dry-Hopped Bitter, a personal favourite. "Peculiar," is somewhat akin to a Scottish ale, dark, malty, and finishing with a touch of sweetness. Their other offering is Keefe's popular Irish Stout.

Somewhat surprisingly, Kentville proved to be the locale for Nova Scotia's second brew pub. The brainchild of Brian Fitzgerald and long-time home brewer Randy Lawrence, Paddy's Pub opened in the spring of 1995. Randy Lawrence has since moved on, and the current brewmaster is Wayne Shankle. The success of Paddy's Pub in Kentville induced Fitzgerald to open a second operation in nearby Wolfville and to move the brewery there as well. Since Wolfville is both a college town and a tourist centre, Paddy's new spot quickly proved as successful as the original. A fire in 2005 caused major damage, but fortunately, the brewery itself remained intact. The renovated pub will reopen shortly.

Paddy's makes a light-bodied Cream Ale, an Annapolis Valley Ale in the bitter English style, and their best-selling Oatmeal Stout. The pub also decided to have fun with Kentville's plague of unwelcome crows and came up with a

The historic
Henry House

Scottish style they named Raven Ale. The beer's slogan is "Kentville is crowing about Raven Ale." During the year, the brewery creates seasonal specialty beers including Honey Wheat Beer, using local honey, Bock and Octoberfest beers, and the strong (7 per cent) Winter Warmer around Christmastime.

Rogue's Roost opened on Spring Garden Road in Halifax in 1998 and has been a popular spot ever since. Brewmaster Lorne Romano had extensive brewing experience in Toronto before settling in Nova Scotia. In his small brewery, which is visible to the clientele, Romano usually has five beers on tap: English Pale Ale, Cream Ale, IPA, Brown Ale, and Rogue's Red are regulars. Other brews are available seasonally. Two other noteworthy Nova Scotia brew pubs are Rudders, located on the Yarmouth waterfront, close to the ferry terminal, and the Rare Bird Pub in Guysborough.

Nova Scotia's two microbreweries came out of the starting blocks at almost the same time, launching their first beers in the early summer of 1997. Propellor Brewery was launched in Halifax by long-time home-brewing enthusiast John Allen. After considering the idea of starting his own microbrewery, John decided that if he didn't start one, someone else would. Having spent many years in the film business as a property master, John perhaps didn't have the typical background for an aspiring microbrewery owner, although he doesn't see it that way. "The movies," he says "are a great preparation for this business. They expect the impossible, and somehow you achieve it." John is an avowed admirer of English beer, and his flagship Pale Ale and Extra Special Bitter are unashamedly full-flavoured English beers.

Propellor Brewery supplies draught beer to many watering holes in HRM, as well as others on the south shore and in Cape Breton. To John's surprise, though, the demand has been higher for more labour-intensive bottled beer.

Propellor launched a new India Pale Ale in 2005, a first-class brew that would shine in any international competition. Currently, it is available only from the brewery's Gottingen Street location.

Having developed his enthusiasm as a home brewer first, former naval officer Brian Titus founded the Garrison Brewery, also in Halifax. Garrison's beer is markedly different from Propellor's, as the Irish Red Ale and Barrack Street Brown Ale are decidedly malty styles; both are available on draught. Since launching, Garrison and Propellor have thrived. Their bottled beers are widely available at Nova Scotia Liquor Corporation outlets around the province. Garrison's speciality beers include a Jalapeno Ale and the coffee-flavoured Khybeer Mocha Ale, available from the brewery. Brian Titus urges consumers to "embrace this explosion of choice and don't be afraid to try new things."

The burgeoning craft beer revolution is adding a great new dimension to the attractions of Nova Scotia. As with wine-making, it adds richness to the local culture, helps tourism, and is a source of new employment. Current brewing regulations were established prior to the microbrewery and brew pub movements and are more reflective of the large brewery environment of the past. Some flexibility in these regulations would be a plus for the industry; otherwise, beer-making in Nova Scotia, like wine-making, has a bright future.

Large party dining room at Five Fisherman restaurant

Restaurants and Inns

As a regional wine culture develops, it stimulates local pride. This, in turn, gets people interested in creating innovative cuisine to match the best regional produce with the local wines. Such patterns have been long-established in Old World regions like Burgundy and Tuscany. Much more recently, similar attempts at matching wine and cuisine have been made here in North America. First came recognition for great California wine, followed by the emergence of great California cuisine. California's success has been followed in other wine-growing regions, including Niagara in Ontario and the Okanagan Valley in British Columbia.

Sometimes, for this kind of synergy to take place, it takes an outsider's perspective to see the potential overlooked by local inhabitants. Such was the case in Nova Scotia. Transplanted American chef Michael Smith, who trained at the prestigious Culinary Institute of America, was the first to really champion Canadian food and wine, with a strong emphasis on Nova Scotia. His achievements, first at The Inn on

Menu:

First Course:

Scallop Seviche

Succulent Digby scallops sliced and marinated in fresh lime, ginger, and jalapeno served with vinegar cucumber and a roasted red pepper chipolte chili purée

New York Muscat, 2002 Domaine de Grand Pré

Second Course:

Marinated Maple Smoked Salmon and Springtime Sprouts

Old Orchard Inn smoked salmon marinated in Cape Breton dark rum and local maple syrup flavoured with fresh basil served on potato and topped with tender springtime sprouts and shoots dressed with a truffle infused olive oil and sherry vinegar

Côte de Bras d'Or Cayuga, 2002 Jost Vineyards

Third Course:

Granite

An intermezzo of refreshing ice made with clear, crisp apple wine made from the harvest of the Annapolis Valley

Theatre of Neptune, Lunenburg County Winery

Fourth Course:

Stuffed Pork Loin with Nova Scotia Blueberries

Oven roasted pork loin stuffed with Martock Glenn Farm wild boar seasoned with sage and rosemary accompanied by green beans with brown butter ad a risotto cake finished with wild blueberry au jus

Baco Noir, 2002 Jost Vineyards

Maréchal Foch Reserve, 2001 Domaine de Grand Pré

Fifth Course:

Trio of Truffles

Delectable handmade chocolate truffles, raspberry panna cota in dark chocolate, Nova Scotian maple ganache in milk chocolate and almond amaretto in white chocolate

Ortega Select Late Harvest, 2001 Domaine de Grand Pré

Birchtown Blackcurrant, Lunenburg County Winery

*Atlantic Wine Symposium 2004 Reception and Gala Dinner
Menu created by Chef Joseph P. Gillis and team.*

Bay Fortune in Prince Edward Island and subsequently at Maple Restaurant in Halifax, inspired a new generation of chefs, increasingly trained in the region, who are bringing fresh dynamism to the restaurant scene around Nova Scotia. Hand in hand with this development, an increasing number of restaurant staff are now locally qualified up to the sommelier level. These professionals are knowledgeable about Nova Scotia wines and happy to include them on their wine lists. Savvy restaurateurs, particularly those in the Annapolis Valley wine region, are catching on to the fact that visitors want to taste the local wines and are featuring them more prominently on their menus.

In Nova Scotia, this is so far happening on a relatively small scale, but the signs of a vibrant future are in the air. Wolfville, in the heart of wine country, is home to a couple of wine establishments that are leading the way. The stately Blomidon Inn, once a nineteenth-century sea captain's house, has for many years been capably run by Jim and Donna Laceby. The Laceby sons, Michael and Sean, are also involved in the business: Nova Scotia-trained Michael is the Blomidon Inn's sommelier, and Sean is the inn's resident chef. The Blomidon's wine list, one of the best in Nova Scotia, has won the coveted Wine Spectator Award for Excellence. Apart from offering an extraordinary range of international wines, the list features some fif-

Donna Laceby in the Blomidon Inn gift shop

teen Nova Scotia wines by the bottle and two by the glass, and are more than fairly priced. Sean Laceby's cooking might be described as country gourmet: satisfying, high-quality cuisine with flare. The Inn is very comfortable and has a warm, welcoming atmosphere. The Blomidon Inn makes a great base for touring the surrounding wine region.

The fine Wolfville restaurant Tempest is the creation of chef-owner Michael Howell, a well-travelled Nova Scotian who settled here because of its proximity to wineries. He is an avid supporter of local wines, working closely with the wineries and cooking exclusively with Blomidon Estate and Domaine de Grand Pré wines. He serves four Nova Scotia wines by the glass and several more by the bottle.

Tempest offers its staff yearly seminars on all the Nova Scotia wineries and they are fully conversant with the wines. Tellingly, Nova Scotia wines make up fifteen per cent of annual sales and thirty-five per cent during the summer tourist season. As has happened in other wine regions, when the number of wineries increases, wine becomes the focus for tourism and with it an expanded hospitality industry and enhanced cultural opportunities.

In Halifax, the bustling Halifax Farmers' Market, which takes place every Saturday morning at the historic Alexander Keith's brewery, is the place to go for fine fresh produce, a host of locally produced gourmet items, Nova Scotia wines, and as often as not, lively entertainment. The wineries have their own allotted space, known as the "Wine Cellar," which provides something of a refuge from the jostling crowd of market-goers. Here, you can taste and buy the wines as you would at the winery itself.

The Little Fish restaurant and oyster bar

The Tempest restaurant in Wolfville

One Halifax restaurant where you can count on an exemplary selection of Nova Scotia wine is the venerable Five Fishermen on Argyle Street. "The Five Fish," as it is sometimes called, gained a Wine Spectator Award of Excellence in 2005. The wine list includes eighteen Nova Scotia offerings, all of which are available by the glass, bottle, or carafe. The list is also shown by region, drawing attention to the distinctive character of wines from the Annapolis and Gaspereau Valleys, the Malagash Peninsula and the Bras d'Or Lakes. Below the Five Fishermen is The Little Fish,

Facing page: Blomidon Inn

MENU:

Scallops with Vanilla,
Lemon Brown Butter

Berkshire Pork Ravioli,
Pumpkin Seed Shadow

"Stutz" Reduction

2003 Petit Rivière Côtes
de Lahave Sur Lie

Free Range Duck Sous-Vide

Mace Savarin, Thyme, and Apple Gel

2003 Jost Trilogy

Fundy Peach and Blueberry Wine Sorbet

Lunenburg County Winery

Truffle and Honey-Glazed Arctic Char

Sweet Corn Flan, Carrot Purée

Leek and Potato Gnocchi

Asparagus and Brussels Sprout Leaves

2005 Domaine de Grand Pré L'Acadie
Blanc Reserve

Vanilla Panna Cotta, Orange Jelly,
Blueberry Strap

Soft Chocolate Cake, Maple Roasted
Nut Ice Cream

Panko Pears, Spiced Syrup

2004 Sainte-Famille Vidal Icewine

*5th annual Taste of Nova Scotia Awards
Dinner 2006*

Halifax Farmers' Market

which includes an oyster bar. In season, you can experience the distinctive flavours of oysters from five or six different Maritime regions washed down with a steely crisp glass of Nova Scotia Seyval or l'Acadie Blanc.

A growing number of restaurants around the province are making a point of serving Nova Scotia wines with Nova Scotia foods. There is a special affinity between the crisp, fresh character of whites, such as l'Acadie and Seyval, with the region's fresh seafoods. Among those, two that stand out are Gabrieau's Bistro in Antigonish and Fleur et Sel in Lunenburg.

WHERE TO BUY NOVA SCOTIA WINES

Each winery has its own on-premises store where the best selection can be obtained. In addition, most of the wineries are represented at the Halifax Farmers' Market. The four private wine stores in the Halifax Metro area also keep a selection of local wines. They are located as follows: The Bishop's Cellar, Bishop's Landing on the Halifax waterfront; Premier Wine and Spirits, City Centre Atlantic, just off Spring Garden Road; Cristall & Luckett, Sunnyside Mall Bedford; VinArt, Bayers Lake.

The Nova Scotia Liquor Corporation's Port of Wines store lists several of the better Nova Scotia wines, some of which may also be found in larger NSLC stores.

APPENDIX
Limited Releases

Nova Scotia wineries are generally small family-owned operations and, except for widely planted varieties like l'Acadie Blanc and Marechal Foch, levels of other varieties tend to be quite limited. Local growers continue to work with a number of grapes that show promise to see how they will fare over the long-term. Viniferas, in particular, have only been produced in very small quantities. These "limited releases" are worth looking out for, as they are of special interest when they can be found.

A number of the wines reviewed below may no longer be available, or the vintages may have changed since I tasted them. These wines are included anyway, as they will give the reader an idea of the individual winery style and the main varieties produced by each. Please note that prices may also have changed since this writing.

BLOMIDON RIDGE BARREL FERMENTED CHARDONNAY, 2003 $18.95. (MAY BE AVAILABLE AT THE HALIFAX FARMERS' MARKET)

Crisp fresh green fruit on the nose is softened by vanilla spice and light traces of oak. Plenty of green apple comes through on the palate with a clean, fresh finish and just a hint of butter. Lighter than most Chardonnays, it is very appealing and will pair well with Nova Scotia seafoods.

BLOMIDON RIDGE BACO NOIR, 2003 $13.99 (MAY BE AVAILABLE AT THE HALIFAX FARMERS' MARKET)

Youthful and purple-coloured with an elegant plum and black cherry bouquet backed by spicy oak and

NOVA SCOTIA VINTAGE CHART

It is far too soon to attempt a definitive vintage chart for all Nova Scotia wines and regions. Many of the most exciting regions have only produced a few vintages from very young vines. The track record is simply too short to come up with meaningful ratings. In the Annapolis Valley region and in the Malagash Peninsula, though, where there is a real history of grape growing, vintage ratings make more sense.

The brief chart below rates Nova Scotia vintages since 1997, for both reds and whites. The ratings are based on the ripeness of the vintage and overall quality. As in all vintages and in all regions of the world, good wine is made in bad years and bad wine is made in good years. Vintage charts, therefore, should be used only as a broad guide. Often, good vineyard management and excellent winemaking can be just as important to the end result.

10 = Excellent

1 = Very poor, avoid

	Whites	Reds
1997	8	7
1998	7	8
1999	7	9
2000	7.5	6
2001	8	9
2002	7	6.5
2003	8	8.5
2004	7	6
2005*	7.5	7

* 2005 ratings are preliminary. The more I have tasted, the better the wines appear to be. I attribute this partly to much improved vineyard practice and winemaking skills.

light, leafy herbal notes. Black cherry and peppery spice flavours and good weight in the mouth offer promise for the future. Needs a couple of years in the cellar to shed youthful acidity. An excellent match for grilled burgers, robust red meats, and firm, nutty cheeses.

JOST VINEYARDS RIESLING, 2004 $14.99

Made from grapes grown on the upper slopes of the Gaspereau Valley, this pale green wine, with a delicate citrus and light mineral bouquet, shows true Riesling character with a distinctive style of its own. Crisp grapefruit flavours backed by lively acidity come through on the palate with a nicely balanced touch of sweetness. It finishes with pleasing peach and apricot freshness, a touch of crisp mineral and soft floral notes. The good depth of flavour, fruity intensity and varietal style make this a real achievement for Nova Scotia winemaking.

JOST VINEYARDS L'ACADIE BLANC, 2003 $12.99

The attractively aromatic bouquet is clean, with grapefruit, some green apple crispness, and soft spicy vanillin. Nicely rounded flavours of citrus and crisp peach move towards some tart grapefruit on the finish, with just a touch of vanilla smoothness. Medium weight and with plenty of flavour, this is a good match for most seafood and white-meat dishes.

GASPEREAU VINEYARDS ROSE, 2004 $14.99

Made from free-run Lucy Kuhlmann and Castel grapes, this salmon pink wine has enticing sweet red berry scents on the nose with light herbal freshness. Strawberry is predominant on the palate with refreshing acidity and appropriately light sweetness for the ripe berry flavours. The aromatic ripe strawberry character lingers on the finish. Excellent as an aperitif or for summer patio picnics. It also worked well for Fraises au Vin (strawberries with wine).

JOST VINEYARDS PINOT NOIR, 2003 $19.99. LIMITED EDITION

Grapes come from the Racca Vineyard, located at Habitant on the shore of the Minas Basin. Aged in French oak barrels, the wine shows good depth of colour and interesting spicy-sweet black cherry and berry fruit on the nose with some light herbal notes. Mouth filling black cherry and rich berry flavours are almost lushly concentrated. Acidity is brisk and tannins are firm, but not overbearing. Fruit, dry spice, and a deft touch of oak linger on the persistent finish. Pinot fans who don't believe we can grow this grape in Nova Scotia should try this one.

JOST VINEYARDS LEON MILLOT, 2003 $13.99. LIMITED EDITION

Deep ruby-coloured with lively red berry, red currant, and fresh herbal scents on the nose, this medium-bodied red has lots of red berry flavour, moderate tannins, and spicy bitter cherry notes on the finish. It has a similar food-friendly character to many Italian reds and will pair well with grilled meats, tomato-based pasta dishes, and firm-ripened cheeses.

JOST VINEYARDS RESERVE MARECHAL FOCH, 2003 $19.99

Estate grown and aged in French oak barrels, deep ruby-coloured in the glass, the bouquet has red berry and spicy/peppery notes, not unlike a Côtes du Rhone. Sweet red berry flavour, moderate tannins and some youthful acidity in the mouth culminate in a nicely integrated berry fruit, spice, and subtle oak finish. Made in a more approachable style than previous vintages, this one will pair especially well with red-meat dishes and grills.